Moulton Library
Bangor Theological Seminary

Charles G. McCully
Fund

Research School
01-00019009 of
Theology
Library

AUTO-BIOGRAPHY

OF

LEMUEL NORTON:

INCLUDING

AN ACCOUNT OF HIS EARLY LIFE — TWO YEARS IN A PRINTING OFFICE — ELEVEN YEARS AT SEA, IN WHICH HE WAS TWICE SHIPWRECKED, AND EXPERIENCED SEVERAL NARROW ESCAPES FROM DEATH.

ALSO

His Christian Experience

AND

LABORS IN THE GOSPEL MINISTRY.

PORTLAND:
ADVERTISER STEAM JOB PRINTING OFFICE,
HORACE C. LITTLE, PRINTER.
1861.

Entered according to Act of Congress, in the year 1861, by
LEMUEL NORTON,
In the Clerk's Office of the District Court of the United States for the District of Maine.

TO THE READER.

HAVING been repeatedly importuned by some of my friends to publish a Memoir of my Life, and hoping that such a book may be of some little use to the church and the world, I have, notwithstanding the many embarrassments under which I labor, endeavored, to the best of my ability, to set before the reader in the following pages a brief narrative of my early life, omitting many things that might be of interest to some, but not t all who might chance to read this book, lest I should weary the patience of those who have but little time to read, and in this way do them more harm than good.

I have endeavored to tell no very lengthy stories in this work, but have been as concise and brief as I could and do justice to the subject under consideration, in all cases having the most sacred regard for truth and urbanity.

Should the critical reader, after examining the following pages, come to the conclusion that there are some things in this book that are not worth the time consumed in reading them, I would only say to such, as was said to one in another case, "Such as I have give I unto thee."

The author barely hopes that this humble effort to contribute something to the glory of God's grace, in his wonderful care over, and astonishing goodness to, one of the most unworthy of all his servants, may influence others to put their trust in Him who is good to all, and whose tender mercies are over all his works.

The account of my Christian experience and call to the Ministry, as well as my subsequent labors in the Gospel Ministry, are very brief and very imperfect, owing in part to the impossibility of calling to mind many important events which took place in the course of my labors, both as an evangelist and as a pastor, and also on account of the amazing cheapness of the book, the subscription price being only fifty cents, which renders it necessary to restrict the number of pages to something less than two hundred.

Not wishing to detain the reader any longer with remarks like these, I will only add that it is my heart's desire and prayer to God, that whoever reads this little book may, after a careful examination of the book and of themselves, come to the conclusion that it has, to say the least, done them some spiritual good.

> Go, little book, and tell the world
> How far your author went astray;
> And sought for happiness and joy
> In hateful sin's delusive way.
>
> Go, tell it, also, of that grace
> Which saved him from all sin and woe;
> And sent him forth to plead with men
> To turn and find salvation too.

THE AUTHOR.

Falmouth, May 17, 1861.

CONTENTS.

CHAPTER I.

BIRTH AND PARENTAGE — FATHER'S HOUSE STRUCK WITH LIGHTNING — ACCIDENT — LAME FOOT — ENTERS THE PRINTING OFFICE — LEAVES AT THE END OF TWO YEARS, ... 7

CHAPTER II.

GOES TO SEA — VOYAGE TO THE WEST INDIES — SICK IN BOSTON — RETURNS HOME AND SPENDS THE WINTER — VOYAGE TO FRANCE — SHORT ALLOWANCE ON PASSAGE HOME — GOES TO NEW YORK WITH CAPTAIN THOMAS M'LELLAN — FROM THERE TO LIVERPOOL — SECOND VOYAGE TO FRANCE — VOYAGE TO INDIA, . . . 19

CHAPTER III.

VOYAGE TO THE WEST INDIES — PRESSED ABOARD A MAN-OF-WAR — HAS THE YELLOW FEVER — GOES TO HONDURAS — CAST AWAY ON THE COAST OF FLORIDA — GOES PRIVATEERING — GETS CLEAR — RETURNS TO BOSTON — FINALLY GOES HOME — ANOTHER VOYAGE TO THE WEST INDIES — LIVERPOOL — WEST INDIES — DISMASTED AT SEA — VOYAGE TO THE WEST INDIES — LIVERPOOL AND FRANCE — RETURNS HOME — SPENDS THE WINTER — GETS MARRIED — MAKES ANOTHER VOYAGE TO EUROPE — SICK BROTHER, ... 51

vi   CONTENTS.

CHAPTER IV.

ONCE MORE TO LIVERPOOL — CAST AWAY — SHIP LOST — LAST VOYAGE TO SEA, ... 85

CHAPTER V.

EXPERIENCES RELIGION — JOINS THE CHURCH — COMMENCES HOLDING MEETINGS — LICENSED TO PREACH — FIRST TEXT — ORDINATION, ... 97

CHAPTER VI.

VISITS VINALHAVEN, ISLESBOROUGH AND MACHIAS,   127

CHAPTER VII.

MOVES TO MOUNT DESERT — BECOMES PASTOR OF A BAPTIST CHURCH — REVIVAL OF RELIGION — BECOMES A FREE WILL BAPTIST — ORGANIZES CHURCHES IN THE VICINITY OF MOUNT DESERT — MOVES TO MONTVILLE PURCHASES A FARM — PREACHES SOME AND FARMS IT SOME — EXPERIENCES A LOSS OF CHILDREN AND WIFE, ... 137

CHAPTER VIII.

REMOVES TO SOUTH MONTVILLE — LOSES ANOTHER DAUGHTER — MARRIES A SECOND TIME — MOVES TO FALMOUTH — VISITS PHILADELPHIA — PREACHES IN SEAMEN'S BETHELS — ADVICE TO YOUTH — CONCLUSION, . . 177

SERMON, ... 187

AUTO-BIOGRAPHY OF LEMUEL NORTON.

CHAPTER I.

I was born in Edgarton, Martha's Vineyard, Mass., June 2, 1785. My parents' names were Noah Norton and Jerusha Dunham. They were of English descent, though both were natives of the beautiful Isle above named. My parents in 1786 moved from Massachusetts to what was then called the district of Maine. I was at that time the youngest of six children. My father, being a house carpenter, found plenty of work in this then almost wilderness part of New England, and took the oversight in building more than fifty dwellings, taking them from the stump and seeing them finished In this way he reared a family of seven sons and three daughters.

Rev. Peter Powers, Congregationalist, was Pastor of the Church of which my parents were members, and of course we were all thoroughly taught the doctrine contained in the Westminister Catechism, which doctrine in those days was considered by the people generally almost as sacred as the Holy Bible itself.

My father's house at the Vineyard stood near a small fresh pond. Not long before they moved into the Eastern Country an incident occurred which I will here mention, because I may have occasion to revert to it again. A terrific thunder storm suddenly sprang up in the night, and so terrible were the flashes of lightning and the rattling of the thunder, that the whole family were aroused and got up, immediately after which, at the request of my mother, my father fell on his knees and commenced praying that God would protect them during this terrible tempest. At this moment, while thus engaged in prayer, the house was struck, the chimney was cleft in two from top to bottom, my mother was knocked down, an infant in her arms was thrown across the room, the two-inch oak plank of which the entry floor was made was shivered into kindling wood, and *every* pane of glass in the house was broken, so that the house was made a mere wreck. Strange as it may appear, in all this fearful catastrophe no lives were lost, though it was weeks before my poor mother got entirely over this terrible shock.

But to return and speak of myself. The first event of my life that I can now call to mind, of any special interest, is that of hearing a sermon preached by the Rev. Daniel Merrill, of Sedgwick, Orthodox, when I was about twelve years of age. This was in the town of Brooksville, then a district in Castine, county of Hancock. This discourse affected me exceedingly, young as I was — so much so that as soon as I returned home I retired by myself and wept profusely; and although that sermon was preached sixty-three years ago, and is so far back in the dim distance, I can distinctly remember this day, February 24, 1861, with what awful solemnity he portrayed the miseries of the lost in hell.

This, however, soon wore off, and I became as mirthful as ever, and used to take delight in showing to other boys of my age how much I could excel them in running, jumping, wrestling, and such like sports, which I now consider to be perfectly innocent, and, indeed, indispensable to the growth and development of children, but, however, should never be indulged in to excess, or at too great an expense for their parents, as is frequently the case

At the age of fourteen I was smart and healthy, and could do as much work as my next older brother, who was about three years the oldest. At this time my father sent me into the field with my scythe one morning to mow, and on coming out where I was at work, observed that what I had done was well done, only I had not done enough to make it profitable either to him or to myself, and in this I perfectly agreed with him; and what was a little singular, this was the first and the last time I ever attempted to mow a single clip till after I was twenty-four years of age. A few days after this little affair took place, an accident befel me, which I now think changed the whole future course of my life.

While chopping wood at the door, I scored in a

stick which required to be chopped off twice to fit it for the four-feet fire-place in the kitchen (the stick or log being about ten inches through), and then stepped over it to stick my axe into one of the scores I had made, in order the more readily to turn it over, and being a little careless of how I struck, I extended the axe so far as to hit the off corner of it against the farther part of the scarf, which caused the ax to glance off a little — just enough to light upon my foot nearest the log — and having put extra force to the axe in order to sink it deep into the log, that it might hold fast so that I could turn the log over by it, it made its terrible way through shoe and stocking, flesh and bone, directly down through the great toe joint of my left foot. It being very warm, the very last of June, and, withal, my blood much heated by chopping, flowed freely from the wound, and caused me to drop my axe and make for the house as fast as possible, on entering which, my poor mother, seeing the blood flow so profusely, became alarmed and cried out: "Have you killed yourself?" I told her no, but that I had spoiled my foot, which indeed, to some extent, proved true. Had the axe gone clear through my foot, it would, no doubt, after proper elapse of time, with good care, notwithstanding the extreme heat of the weather in July, have healed up sound. But not so; it did, indeed, heal up, but not sound; and after fifteen days' suffering, and my foot having become nearly as thick as two feet, I had to call in a physician and have it opened from my ankle joint to the second joint of my great toe. In twenty days from the time I struck this almost fatal blow I was carried five miles to Dr. Mann's house, in Castine village, where I remained twenty days more under his hands, during all which time I had the best possible care taken of me, not only by the doctor and his family, but by the young lady whose entire business it was to anticipate my wants, and to see that they were all supplied.

At the end of the twenty days at the doctor's, my wound being about healed and my health being otherwise pretty good, the doctor thought it would be safe for me to return home, though not exactly as I went, he having a desire to let the villagers see that he had made a cure of me, compelled me, or rather insisted on my walking with crutches to the boat at the end of Main street, in which I was received and returned joyfully home to my father's house, where I was gladly received. But notwithstanding my wound was about healed up, yet there remained thirty days' more suffering for me before I would be considered well. My foot, not having been exercised for forty days, became entirely helpless, so that I could make no use of it whatever, not so much as to let it rest on the floor without being in perfect agony, and when I attempted to bear the least weight upon it, it would feel as though thousands of hot needles were being pierced through and through the whole of it. I had become so used to going with my crutches that it became a kind of second nature, and so I moved on in this way till my friends became almost discouraged about me. At last, however, one morning when I was about rising, I overheard my father say that he was almost discouraged about my ever walking again. My mother also expressed about the same. This made me feel very sad, and I determined that day to make some extraordinary effort to use my foot again. Accordingly after breakfast, in company with my younger brother, I went out into the field on my crutches some fifteen or twenty rods, stopped and turned round, looking at the house, and a thought struck my mind like this, to take my crutches, and one at a time throw them as far towards the house as I could, and then put down my foot and walk back to the house, let it cost me whatever amount of pain it might. I made the attempt, and succeeded beyond all expectation, walking straight off to the house, limping but very little, and picking up my crutches as I went, the children who were with me crying out, "See him walk! See him walk!" Indeed, the whole family rejoiced, but none so much as myself. This put an end to the use of crutches with me. I laid them by, and have never used them since. In a few days my limb gathered strength, so that notwithstanding I had lost the use of the great toe joint, it having become entirely stiff, I could walk several miles in a day.

About this time a newspaper had just been started in the village of Castine — the only village of any considerable importance east of Wiscasset, in the district of Maine. This paper was then called the Castine Gazette and Eastern Advertiser, David Jones Waters, Editor, and was at this time the only paper printed east of Wiscasset in Maine. In it was an advertisement for an apprentice, and I being about fourteen years of age, and in other respects answering the description given in the advertisement tolerably well, and the physician saying I could never walk over five miles in a day, it was agreed on all sides that I should be a printer. And accordingly in the Autumn of 1799 I went into the printing office and commenced type-setting. A little before this, some young gentlemen and ladies had called in to see this new establishment in their neighborhood, and how it was that newspapers are printed, and in their passing round among the cases of type, or in some of their movements, they managed to upset a case of type so that they were piled all up together topsy-turvy, making what printers denominate pi. It was my first work to set these on end, so that they could the more readily be distributed into their proper places in the case.

In a very few months I became quite a proficient in type-setting, which business I liked very much, because it learned me rapidly how to read and how to spell. And here let me just say, that printers are the best spellers of any class of people in the world, lawyers themselves not excepted.

Here I am now in my new relation, the youngest of two apprentices, the other, Ebenezer Whitney, being about nineteen. And being the youngest, I had every week, on the day on which the paper was published, to take some seventy-five or a hundred under my arm and pass through every street, leaving a paper at every subscriber's door, or throwing it in at the door. Nothing worthy of note took place with us — everything moved on harmoniously until toward the last of December, when the sad tidings of the death of General George Washington came to our village. This seemed to make every one sad; the whole nation was clad in mourning; we all wore black crape on the right arm for thirty days, as expressive of our grief for the loss of the Father of our Country, who died December 14, 1799, aged sixty-seven years.

Our district of country was so thinly settled in those times, and readers were so scarce, that notwithstanding our paper circulated in quite a number of counties, our subscription list never rose higher, while I was in the office, than from seven hundred and fifty to eight hundred.

In the winter of 1800, my master being short of funds to meet the demands made upon him for paper, ink, etc., sent me up the Penobscot River with bills against subscribers to the amount of about one hundred and fifty dollars. Taking my journey on horseback, the roads being very bad in those days, I passed up the river as far as Coulliard's Ferry, so called, and crossed over on to the west side of the river into Frankfort, and made my way up the river, finding about one house to every one hundred acres. In crossing what is now called Kenduskeag stream, my horse broke through the ice just as I was making the opposite shore, which came very near costing me my life and the life of my beast too, and would no doubt have done so had he not been a very powerful beast, and by much effort rearing up his fore feet on to the ice and breaking it down, we made our way on to terra firma, having been thoroughly drenched in the waters of the Penobscot, At night I arrived safe at the house of General Crosby, where I found an excellent family and pleasant home, right about where the centre of the city of Bangor now stands. In this neighborhood there might have been a house to every fifty acres — not more certain, perhaps not that. I went up as far as Sunkhayze and crossed over on the ice to Edington, and returned through Orrington, Bucksport, Orland and Penobscot, to Castine, having been absent about five days and collected about one hundred dollars, which was considerable in those days. And here I would remark that there were many excellent farms on the margin of this beautiful river. About this time Mr. Waters was appointed deputy sheriff of the County of Hancock, and moved into the jail, hired a housekeeper, and kept house in that part assigned for the turnkey. This brought me into close connection with the prisoners, as I had to carry them their food and pass it in through a square place in the door made for that purpose.

Among the prisoners was one by the name of James Budge, a man forty-five years of age, who was brought down the river from Bangor, who owned a large part of the land on which the city now stands. This Major

Budge, as he was called, was a notorious drunkard and dangerous man, so much so that his wife swore her life against him and had him put in prison.

This man, by the help of a knife and a file, had taken off the sheet iron of the door and dug a hole almost through large enough for him to pass out; this I happened to discover by seeing a few of his scattered chips on the floor of his cell, which led me to pass round outside of the prison, where I discovered the whole work, where this man had labored for weeks till he had got a pile of hacks or small chips, as large as a winrow of hay, as much as ten or twelve feet long, which he had taken from the cavity above named, and would no doubt have effected his escape that night had it not been for the two or three pieces of fragments discovered on the floor which led to his detection. When the sheriff went in, sword in, hand he was dreadful loth to give up and lose all his labor; but it was no use; the glittering steel seemed to alarm him, and he finally yielded, to take lodgings in more secure abode for the future, though he looked fearfully at me as he passed by, supposing that I was his detector. Some weeks after this, having greatly improved and become humble and penitent, his friends came and took him out of prison and carried him home to Bangor, where I suppose he has long since paid the debt of nature and gone to his final resting place. He was a man of strong intellectual powers, rather a good scholar, and something of a poet; wrote a great deal, — made some excellent poetry, — but rum, that demon rum, which destroys its thousands every year, destroyed him, got the mastery over him, and entirely ruined him for this world, and probably for that which is to come.

Being rather of an intellectual turn of mind, I enjoyed the business of printing very much, became strongly attached to the man with whom I lived, and should no doubt have continued with him, had it not been that I had an unconquerable desire to see more of the world than I possibly could while confined within the walls of a printing office. Ships, brigs and schooners coming in from different parts of the world and anchoring in the harbor, within hailing distance of our office, from time to time, greatly attracted my attention, and their splendid appearance with the men and boys on the yards and at the mast-head furling and sometimes loosening their sails, drew my affections quite away from all other pursuits, and I longed to be a sailor. My roving propensities overcame me, and I finally came to the conclusion that I would leave the indoor work of setting type, and go and see what was to be seen in other climes and in other kingdoms.

In order to gratify this insatiate desire, which at times became almost unendurable, the first thing to be accomplished was to obtain my freedom, for I was bound as strong as my indentures could bind me to serve till I was twenty-one years of age, being now but sixteen, and five years still ahead to serve. This, however, I accomplished, by getting my oldest brother to settle up with Mr. Waters, paying him all the cash down for my time, and taking my notes, young as I was, for his security.

After settling up in the above described manner with my master, for his sake, whom I so much esteemed, and whom I so well loved, I consented to stay a few months with him and set types, till he could procure help in this emergency, for emergency it was; for type-setters in those days were hardly to be found east of the Kennebec. This business being all amicably adjusted, I packed what little I had of clothing, together with a Bible and Watts' Hymns, and leaving my father's house went on board the good schooner Polly, of Castine, belonging to Capt. Joseph Perkins, of said place, where a birth had been provided for me to go as cook to the West Indies.

CHAPTER II.

HERE was the commencement of my sea-faring life, which began in June, 1801. The first few days out I was very sick, but not at all sick of the voyage. I had started, and I felt determined to go through, and know what it was to be a sailor. Nothing worth naming occurred until one day the crew were called upon to see who could jump the farthest; and after a while I was invited to try my skill in this way for their amusement. After making several leaps as far on the smooth deck as I conveniently could, the captain and mate insisted on my trying it once more, which, to please them, I consented to do; but while taking my position for that purpose they contrived, unnoticed by me, to throw grease on the deck where they supposed I should land, and having made an unusual effort to jump as far as possible, and striking the deck where they had made it slippery, my feet glanced from under me and I came down with great force flat on the deck, hurting me considerably, and making fine sport for them to see how completely they had succeeded in their attempt to play this joke upon me; however, I picked myself up as well as I could and went about my work, leaving them to their own reflections. I do not think they meant any harm toward me, for they were very clever men, and always kind to me and to all on board. Not long after this it came into my head to return the joke — in a very moderate way, to be sure; when they were all hands below in the cabin, out of the sun, which by the way was very hot in these latitudes, and it being about calm, I thought I would give them a sudden start, which I did by violently hauling in the shark hook which was towing astern with a piece of beef in order to catch some of these man-eaters if possible, with which the sea seemed to be so abundantly supplied. This gave them a sudden start; on deck with haste they came, and on seeing the hook and the beef and no shark, they of course were not a little chagrined; however, they put up with it better than I expected, and returned below to finish their dinner, while I was whistling away at the helm, a light breeze having sprang up in the mean time. The next joke worth naming was on the day we made land, the Island of Martinico. After getting into the latitude of this Island we ran due west a number of days, with fair winds and fresh breezes. The day we made this Island the captain, and mate too, inquired of me if I did not think it a wonderful thing to find in the midst of the ocean so small an object, to which I rather incautiously replied I thought it was, but that they had been considerable time looking for it. This, to be sure, was rather impudent for a boy of sixteen summers only, to say to the captain of a West Indiaman and here I will only say that I advise all boys who may chance to read this book to be very careful how they speak, and how they answer those who are superior to them in years and station.

We were soon safe moored in the harbor of St. Piers, where our cargo of boards were easily disposed of for fifty dollars per thousand. This was a beautiful village, and the first I ever saw except my own beloved Castine. There were thousands of sable Africans sweating under the heat of a vertical sun, toiling for their white masters, who were regaling themselves in the shade, and faring sumptuously every day. The first of this colored race who attracted my attention especially, was the bowman of a boat's crew that came along side soon after we came to anchor. The chain attached to a ring about his neck was about the size of a common ox-chain, and about four feet in length; the ring round his neck was suitable for an ox-yoke; he rowed the bow oar, used the boat hook to hold the boat and keep it from chafing against the vessel, and to shove the boat off when ordered to do so, all which he did with the most perfect ease and exactness, notwithstanding his ring and chain, a few links of which I noticed he contrived to hold up with his left hand when he had nothing else to do. The ring was made with a hinge, which would open wide enough to receive his neck and then close and fasten with a key. His person had such a dignity about it, and his whole appearance was such, that it made an impression on my youthful heart never to be erased while life shall last; and now while I write, notwithstanding that scene was presented to my view nearly

sixty years ago, it is as fresh in my memory as though
it had taken place but a few days since. He was
stout, portly, dignified, and manly in his appearance
— so much so that I was led to say to a bystander,
"he looks like a king." He was so desirous of freedom, I was told, that he had ran away several times,
but was as often caught again, and had this chain put
on him to prevent any further trouble in that direction. I was told, also, that a fifty-six, or some other
heavy article, was attached to this chain when his
work was done at night, to make sure where he would
be found in the morning. Here for the first time I
saw the tall tamarind tree, the orange and the lime
trees, the pine apple, the plantain, the bananna, the
sour sop, and all manner of tropical fruits in abundance; here, too, was the beautiful cane fields, in one
of which I saw some fifty slaves (for this was a land
of bondage then, though since made free), all standing
in a row with hoe in hand, all striking at once, turning over the rich and fertile soil (I believe there were
no oxen or plows there then) and making it ready for
the reception of the seed; here, too, were the lofty
mountains and deep vallies, running brooks and crystal streams; here, too, was the refreshing sea-breeze
—just as sure to come as the day; also the warm
zephyr from the mountain-top at night — all which
are so exhiliarating and comfortable as almost to make
one forget his own northern home, and have a desire
to remain here forever.

Our lumber being all out, hold swept and made

ready, we commenced taking in our homeward-bound cargo, consisting principally of molasses, in hogsheads, one of which we lost the most of on account of the cleat giving way which held the fall with which we hoisted the cargo on board and lowered it into the hold; this like to have ruined the young man's hands who was holding on to the fall; the cleat giving away suddenly, he had no chance to let go the rope, but was strung up some ten or fifteen feet in the air, the rope all the while running through his hands with swiftness, scorching them most fearfully; the hogshead, falling into the hold, out goes a part of the head; and the mate, springing into the hold, called out for a bucket, and dipped up molasses, bilge water, and the like, and soon had the cask full, coopered, and stowed as though nothing had happened, except that he put a mark on it so that it might be known from other casks on our arrival home.

Soon after this we weighed and sailed again for home, and after a very pleasant passage arrived safe in Castine, after an absence of about eight weeks.

After discharging our cargo, which was done in a few days, and handing over to my brother what I could spare of the effects of my voyage, I soon left for Boston in pursuit of a voyage, but business being very dull, I was obliged to work about the wharves with what was then called lumpers, at loading and unloading vessels, etc. This was in the autumn of 1801. By eating too freely of fruit I was thrown into a fever, and being among entire strangers I suffered some for

for want of proper care. Dr. Thomas, to whom I applied for assistance, was very good to me, not asking anything for his services, but Mrs. Fish, the woman where I boarded in Fore Street, was very hard with me, charging four dollars per week for my board; although I was very weak, I always kept about house, and had no attention from any one during the long wearisome nights I spent alone in my chamber. One Sunday morning I walked away down on to one of the wharves, and was so weak and tired that I laid down on the wharf to rest before attempting to return to the house, and while lying there weak as a little child, a gentleman passed by to the end of the wharf, and on returning spoke to me and said, "What are you lying there for, you miserably drunken young man." I replied I was not drunken, as he seemed to think, but was sick, and was resting in order to get strength that I might walk back to the house where I boarded; this was the first and last that I ever saw or heard of him, or ever wish to. I thought he lacked two things instead of one, that is to say, Christian charity and human kindness.

After being sick some three or four months with a slow fever, occasioned entirely for want of taking proper care of myself in relation to my diet, I began slowly to recover. Soon after this my brother, to whom I was indebted for my freedom, arrived in Boston from Liverpool, who came immediately to see me, and glad I was to see him once more in the land of the living. He put me on board the ship John and Phebe, of Castine, bound to Castine, where I arrived safe home, after an absence of perhaps five or six months, having accomplished nothing except this: I had learned something of the importance of taking care of my health. I spent the winter at home, attended the district school, and chopped my father's firewood, enjoying myself well among my former associates.

In the spring of 1802, Capt. David Larrabee, who married our sister, and who was going to France in the brig Federal Volunteer, wrote to my brother and I to come to Portland and go with him, which we accordingly did. We had a pleasant passage out to Bayonne, in the Bay of Biscay, where we discharged our cargo of masts, spars, and oar rafters. This is a very ancient city: here is the very seat of the French Revolution, here is to be seen the framework of the old guillotine, and the place about ten feet high where the bodies of those innocent victims were laid with their heads on the block, where the terrible knife came down from above them and severed with one fatal blow the head from the body of many thousands, simply because they would not become traitors to their king and his despotic power. Here, also, blood was poured out like water, and saturated the ground all around this infernal machine; here also may be seen the tree of liberty, standing erect and spreading its long and beautiful branches out in every direction, as the emblem of protection to all who took shelter under its shadow. Streets lined with beggars are met with in this place; here is where I saw for the first time any of this class of human beings, to whom I immediately gave about all the money I had, and then felt as though my heart would break for these poor suffering creatures. I returned on board the brig and asked the captain for more money, and when told that I had given the most of it to the beggars (which was about nine shillings) he refused letting me have any more for that purpose. Here we took in freight for Lisbon, Portugal, and on our way stopped at a place in Spain called Bilboa, where we took on board more freight. Bilboa is at the entrance of the Bay of Biscay, and is remarkably picturesque, on account of its Mountainesses, and when passing in by the fort, the soldiers with their muskets on its walls seemed but little larger than pigeons. Here our captain went to see what is called the bull fight, where thousands collect together to see this barbarous and cruel battle among the brute beasts, where one or more are sure to lose their lives. From this place we sailed to Lisbon. This is a large city, the largest and greatest place for commercial business of any in Portugal. There we landed our freight, or rather put it into lighters, who took it on shore for us, there being no keys here for large vessels to lay along side of to discharge their cargoes.

Deeply laden with salt, we left this place for Portland, with a very scanty store of provisions, and had it not been for a small supply we obtained of a vessel bound to England, on the Grand Banks, we must inevitably have perished or suffered exceedingly for the want of food; as it was, we cooked and ate the last morsel we had off Seguin, ten leagues at sea from the city of Portland. Having a strong breeze and free, in a few hours we arrived safe into port, after a stormy passage of almost continued head winds, in about seventy-five days, having been absent from home about six months.

The effects of this voyage enabled me, with what I had previously paid my brother, to square up with him, with a very small exception, which I paid him some four years after.

In the fall of 1802, having been in Portland some two or three weeks, I again, in company with my brother, concluded to take another voyage across the Atlantic to Europe. Accordingly, we shipped on board the new ship Cornelia, Capt. Thomas McLellan, Master, bound first to New York, and thence to Belfast, in Ireland. On our way to New York we encountered a severe gale, and for some purpose or other we anchored off Long Island, not very far north of the Highlands of Neversink, commonly so called; here it was very rough; our best bower anchor had enough to do to hold us from drifting. At last orders were given to get the ship under way. Preparations being made, we commenced heaving ahead, but before much was accomplished in gathering in the cable, the post which sustained the entire pressure of the polls that held the windlass, and saved all that was gained by heaving, gave way, so far as to let the windlass whirl round with rapid force, and the cable, as a consequence, running out of the hawse-hole with great violence, When this took place it threw every man head first over the windlass, and broke and smashed to pieces nearly every handspike in the windlass, there being some eight or nine of them in there at the time. The appearance of things to me (who at that time was holding on to what is called the jig, and consequently was not thrown over the windlass with the others) was most ludicrous, seeing the men piled up there, handspikes smashed up, the captain crying out "All hands to the stoppers," produced in me a sensation which ended in loud laughter, which so provoked him that, had he stood near me, I think he would have knocked me down; but I took care and kept out of his way as much as I could until his anger had abated.

I have named this folly of mine that others may shun such an unwise and impudent course, for impudent it was, considering the condition of things around me. Another thing I would mention as a caution to young men who are about shipping to go a voyage to sea: never ship for able seamen until you are such. Better have two or three dollars a month less wages, than to have full wages at the expense of harmony and justice.

Having been a voyage to the West Indies, and quite a lengthy one to Europe, and being considerable active withal, I ventured to ship as an able seaman, because I knew I could, as the saying is, knot and splice, hand reef and steer; but I soon found that there were many things to be done on board this new ship that I was quite unacquainted with; indeed, I ought to have shipped for an ordinary seaman, if not a green hand. After this the sea gradually became smoother, so that we finally got under way, and soon arrived at New York.

Seamen's wages at this time being very low in New York, we soon perceived that the captain was not very careful about retaining the good will of the crew, but had about as lief they would leave the ship as not. Accordingly several of us did leave, and I among the rest. My brother, however, remained and went the voyage.

Soon after this I shipped on board the good ship Logan, of New York, Captain Mason, of Hudson, commander, bound to Liverpool, laden with cotton. We had a very rough passage out; while scudding before the wind, under a close-reefed main-top-sail and reefed foresail, a sea struck the ship in the stern with such violence that it stove the stern boat almost into kindling wood, leaving little else but the keel, stem and stern port in the davies, driving one of the two men at the wheel into the main rigging, where he caught hold of the shrouds and saved himself, and making a fair break over the ship, so that some of the crew, who were on deck at the time and saw this fearful roller coming, ran up the fore rigging to avoid being engulfed in this frightful wave. Immediately after the ship had risen and shook herself clear of this monster, by the skilful management of our experi-enced commander, she was brought to under a close-reefed main-top-sail, under which she laid too like a duck, and instead of flying before wind and sea with the greatest possible precipitancy, like a frightened foe from a pursuing enemy, she now being turned about, faced both wind and sea, and rode out the gale with almost astonishing ease and safety, except now and then she would roll fearfully and almost dip her long yard arms into the sea, as she gently slipped from it into the gulf beneath.

Three days we lay too as above described, with a fair wind, not daring to put the ship before the wind, on account of the terrible violence of the waves during this westerly gale, or rather hurricane.

I have heard it said that in the winter of 1802 thirteen sail of ships were lost, I think from New England, in attempting to cross the Atlantic to Europe; at any rate, it was a terrible cold and stormy winter; we arrived safe, however, in Liverpool, after a passage of about thirty days.

Soon after getting safe into dock, the doctor came on board, and inoculated such of us as had never had the small pox. Nine days from this time I found myself suddenly seized with a violent pain in the back; so severe was it that I had to quit work and go on shore up to my boarding house; for all hands had to live on shore in this place, none being allowed to use fire, except in a safe lantern, with at least half an inch of water in the bottom of it. Here we had to submit to a law in the custom house, which was under solemn oath to swear, with Bible in hand, that we were native born Americans, and then, to make it more sure, we had to kiss the book. Very many thousands, no doubt, have kissed this same Bible, perhaps many of them foreigners, who had never seen America till they had crossed the Atlantic.

The small pox gave me rather a severe time of it, especially the symptoms, which I thought were more painful than the thing itself.

We left Liverpool after discharging our cargo and taking in freight for New York, and sailed to the South till we took the trade winds, which always blow from the East; we had a pleasant passage home, and arrived sometime in the spring of 1803.

Not long — perhaps a few weeks — after our arrival in New York I sought another voyage. This was done by going down to the wharves and noticing what vessels had a long pendant flying at their main royal mast head. This was a signal that they wanted hands. Seeing a beautiful brig nearly ready for sea lying at the end of the wharf, I signed the shipping papers as an able seaman, a position which I found myself fully able to sustain, and that without any difficulty. This brig was called the Mary, George Main, Commander, and was bound to Bordeaux, in France. This being in the summer, it was of course a very pleasant voyage. We had a few passengers, among whom was the captain's wife, a New York lady of much refinement and good sense. We made our passage to Bordeaux in about forty days. Nothing very special occurred on board our vessel till after our arrival in this city.

Our first mate was some inclined to intemperance, and after the captain and his lady had taken up their abode on shore he (the mate) grew worse, so that in a few days he became unfit for anything except a mad-house, and was absolutely dangerous, threatening to shoot any one who happened to displease him. Things went on in this way for some days, and had it not been that we had rather a steady, good sort of a man for a second mate, things would have been in a worse condition than they were. The captain coming on board one afternoon, discovered at once that all was not right, especially in reference to putting the cargo into the lighters that came along side to receive it. Bags of allspice, and other valuable spices, were carelessly handled, and broke open and scattered about deck without being sewed up and taken care of as they should have been. This appearance of things, together with some information from the second mate, so enraged the captain that he immediately ordered Mr. Kemper to pick up his things and make ready to be set on shore. The boat was soon manned, and our first officer — whom we all loved, being a clever man and well able to do his whole duty with honor to himself and profit to his owners only when he had taken too much of the accursed thing — was by the captain peremptorily ordered into the boat, which order he very reluctantly obeyed. But remonstrance was of no avail. The captain was inexorable, and poor man, he had to leave the brig in a foreign land, among strangers. Oh! how I felt for that poor unfortunate as I helped pull the boat to the shore. We landed him on the beach (for there are no wharves there) and took our leave of him with sadness. Oh! that cruel monster alcohol, how many strong men have been slain by it. Heaven have mercy on our race, and hasten the day when to make or sell any of that body and soul-destroying article, shall be considered a crime, and the same penalty attached to it that there is to the sale of any other poison with a view to destroy life. Some few days after this, Mr. Kemper was seen by some of the crew on shore, but I never saw him after he left the brig.

Now the duty of the first officer devolved on the second, which made it harder for us all. We got on very well, however, each one seeming disposed to do what he could to lighten the burden of the second mate, who now acted as both first and second officer.

Bordeaux is a great commercial city, situated on the western shore of the river Gironde, about sixty miles from the sea. We happened to be here on Bonaparte's birth-day, when all the shipping in the river was decorated with colors flying from every mast head, yards manned, drums beating, cannon roaring, soldiers marching, fire-works, rockets by thousands were sent up sky high, etc., etc.

As I feel it to be my duty, in giving to the world a correct history of my life, to write not only the good, but also the bad, so that the reader may have a fair and accurate account of my whole life. And in order to do this, I will here relate a little affair that took place with me while in this port. One morning a bomb boat came along side about breakfast time with certain things for sale, among which was French brandy. It came into my head to try how much brandy I could drink; not because I was fond of it, for I never liked it half so well as rum, but somehow or other I wanted to experiment with it, and told the man in the boat to pour me out a pint of brandy, handing him at the same time a tin pot to pour it into; this I took and drank all down without taking it from my mouth; I wonder it did not strangle me, but it did not. I however soon began to feel stupid, and fell asleep on the forecastle under the awning placed there to keep the sun off. Here I lay, perhaps an hour or more, utterly unconscious, when the first thing I knew I found myself being drenched from head to foot with water from the draw-bucket in the hands of the mate. I immediately picked myself up as well as I could and went about my work, not a little astonished that I should feel so little affected by such a fearful dose of cogniac. Many a time have I thought of the awful presumption of that hour, and I now think that Divine compassion interposed in my behalf and influenced the mate to throw that water upon me, thus counteracting the influence of the strong drink and so saved me from an awful death. Since that time I have never had any partiality for brandy.

While lying in Bordeaux we painted our beautiful brig all over new, so that she was about the handsomest vessel in port.

The time now arrived when orders came to bend the sails and get ready for sea. These orders were joyfully received, and as cheerfully obeyed, inasmuch as we had been laying here quite as long as any of us wished to. Soon after this we found ourselves out on the Bay of Biscay, headed towards the broad Atlantic. When we came to set the watch (as it is technically called) the captain inquired of me if I would consent to become the second mate, as we had none, and so take charge of the starboard watch, saying if I did so he would take me into the cabin, where I should sit at the same table with the after-guard, so to speak, besides having three or four dollars a month added to my wages. To all this I replied: "No sir; I am the youngest seaman on board, and besides this I have no knowledge of navigation." However, I took charge of his watch and did the best I could.

On the homeward bound passage we had pleasant weather and gentle breezes from the west, which occasioned our passage to be very long — I should think about seventy-five days.

Nothing worthy of remark took place during the passage, that I now recollect, except a difficulty which took place between myself and the steward, who was as black as the ace of spades. This happened one day at noon, or a little after. The captain, mate, and three passengers being below, and the steward also, I took it into my head to see what was in the galley that might be toothsome, having noticed feathers flying about the hen-coop the evening before; the very first glance of my expectant eye discovered the beautiful leg of a fat duck, done nicely brown, lying under the cook's bench in a clean blue and white plate. This was too much for me. I could see no positive reason why I should not have a bit as well as darkey, whom I well knew had made the deposit for his own tooth. Rats, to be sure, were somewhat plenty below deck, but seldom if ever seen above deck at noon-day. All hands being forward of the windlass taking dinner except the man at the wheel, I secured the prize and was finishing the last sweet morsel just as Sambo's head hove in sight coming on deck. To escape by fraud or flight was impossible — take it I must. I knew his head was hard, and it shone like a glass bottle in the sun, but, as good luck would have it, I knew his mode of warfare, and prepared myself for the battle. Along comes Cuffee, anticipating his choice leg of duck with much gusto, and stooping down to see if all was right under the bench, starts back with astonishment to see the empty plate — unmoved, but minus the choice leg.

Now comes the important enquiry: "Who's been into the camboose house since steward been below?" "Why? what's the matter, steward?" "What's de matter, ha? de tief been here and took my dinner." "Rats, rats," respond several voices; but Sambo is not to be put off so. He puts the question most seriously: "Who be dat rascal who took my piece of duck?" Norton now views it but fair, in order to clear all the rest, to make the fearful disclosure, and acknowledge that he took the duck. Accordingly I observed that, passing by the galley I saw in a plate a piece of duck. This was enough. The die was cast, and I must abide the consequences. Passing by me as I stood at the windlass, quick as thought he grabbed me by the two shoulders and brought his head with such force against mine as would have prostrated me on the deck had it not been for the windlass, against which I leaned. I now took my stand back to the windlass, facing the negro, who drew back from me some eighteen or twenty feet, struck into a run, and when within about four or five feet of me would leap and come head first at me with awful swiftness. But Young America's arm was too strong, and his fist too heavy for the sable African, and after three attempts in this way, finding that a blow from his antagonist against the side of his wooly head, at the right time and in the right way, so completely passed him by, giving the windlass the privilege of receiving the butt, and finding the rule in this case to be "let the hardest fend off," he of course found it did not pay, and consequently gave over the struggle. In any other way of contesting our strength I could have whipped two of him; but his head was his defence, and that it was I took care to pass by and let the windlass bring him up. Before I dismiss this affair, let me just say to the reader that negroes have thick skulls and strong necks. Beware of them, and keep them in their place.

Arrived in New York in the Fall of 1803, stopped

on shore a number of weeks, and then took another voyage for France in the brig Friends' Adventure, of New York, bound for Bordeaux, to which place we arrived not while I was in the brig. Having on board a number of French gentlemen, who had sold their estates in the West Indies, and were then homeward bound by the way of New York, on account of the war then existing between France and England, we were suspected of being French property; consequently, when entering the British Channel, we were boarded by an English privateer and taken to Portsmouth, in England, where we were detained — I know not how long — awaiting our trial.

Portsmouth is one of the largest naval stations in England, and is generally thronged with men-of-war of the largest class — such as are termed line-of-battle-ships. Here, too, expeditions are often fitted out in time of war in great haste. On these occasions press gangs patrol the streets by night and by day, utterly regardless of whom they meet, if his hand is hard, which they immediately ascertain by feeling of his palm. Whether he be English, Dutch, Spanish, French, or American, it makes no difference — away he must go to the watch-house and be examined, and if unable to prove his identity or satisfy the recruiting officer that he is not an Englishman, protection or no protection, he the next morning is marched down to the boat and taken on board some ship of war, and ere he is aware he finds himself on the high seas in the midst of battle and war, surrounded with carnage and death. This was certainly true in 1803. Things however differ now, in 1861. Jackson, at New Orleans behind the cotton-bags, in the war of 1812 gave this business a terrible shaking, so that American seamen, peaceably walking the streets in England, are not to be molested with impunity.

Here in Portsmouth and Gosport are any amount of munitions of war — strong forts with their bristling cannon, round, double-headed, and chain shot, together with grape and canister shot are here, with vast magazines of powder awful to think of, which if they should chance to be ignited would, I suppose, shake these beautiful cities nearly all to pices. Here I was pressed three times in one evening, and as often eluded their grasp, owing to my protection, which the officer, strange to say, always respected and let me go. But I did not like this business, for I knew not how soon an expedition might be called for by the king, and then if pressed I might have to go. Hence I concluded to leave the brig and make the best of my way to some place of greater safety.

Being on shore one evening in company with some other sailors, an American captain, whose ship lay off some ten or twelve miles from this at a place called Cowes, in the British Channel, came into the hotel who wanted some two or three hands to go with him to India. I consented at once to go, for four pounds sterling per month, to China. Accordingly next morning I took my chest and hammock into a boat sent for the purpose, bid adieu to the Friend's Adventure, and went on board the beautiful ship Anthony Mangin, of Philadelphia, bound to China, Gustavus Tailor, Commander. This was a fine ship indeed. Every thing on board was done after man-of-war fashion — indeed, she in some sense was a man-of-war, carrying cannon in both waists, and two stern chasers on the taff rail. We left England on the thirteenth of November, and arrived in Batavia on the nineteenth of March, 1804, after a passage of one hundred and twenty-seven days; and what was a little singular, to my knowledge we never saw but one vessel during all that passage across about one hundred degrees of latitude and equally as many of longitude. We sailed from fifty north to about fifty south latitude, in order to take the advantage of the monsoon trade winds, which always blow south-westerly. When crossing the equinoctial line, according to an ancient custom we were bound to have some fun. At noon, when the ship was exactly upon the line which divides the northern from the southern hemisphere, she was hove too, top-gallant sails, royals, and stay sails furled, courses hauled up with the after yards thrown aback, so that the ship lay almost as still as a little island in the midst of the sea.

Now commenced the work of what was called shaving. All who had never crossed the line before were ordered below. A man, trumpet in hand, on the farthest end of the flying jib boom, to represent the fabled Old Neptune, now hails: "Ship ahoy!" "Hilloa!" answers an officer from the quarter deck.

"What ship is that, where from, and by whom commanded?" vociferates the pretended Old Neptune. Old Neptune is now invited on board, with his old tarpaulin hat and miserable old pea jacket, all covered over with barnacles, as if he had been for months under water, and begins to inquire if there are any on board who have never been this way before, and on being informed that there are, has them called up from below and one after another fastened to a gun carriage and shaved by some one of the crew appointed for that purpose to officiate as barber. This is done by putting on the lather, which is obtained from the hen coop, with some old tar brush, and then it is scraped off with a piece of rusty iron hoop, when several buckets of water are thrown over the individual to wash all off clean, and then he is prepared to join in the sport and take a part in shaving the others. The questions put and answered by each perhaps it will be as well not to name just now, only that each one promises never to row when they can sail, never to eat brown bread when they can get white, never to walk when they can as well ride, with many other frivolities not worth naming.

We now made sail again, but soon found ourselves in what was called the calm latitudes, where for days and nights we had not wind enough to fill our lightest sails; the face of the sea as smooth as glass, except the gentle rise and fall of the broad waves, which were occasioned by winds at a distance. Here we lay some ten or a dozen days and nights almost entirely motionless on the bosom of the great blue deep, with nothing to be seen but the clear blue sky above and the vast expanse of water beneath, with a vertical sun shining down upon us as hot as a piece of iron that has been laying very near the fire.

At last, when hope began to flag and expectation perish, what sailors call cat's paws began to appear in the distance. Soon our light sails begin to fill, all hands with pleasing emotions are looking aloft to see the top sails and top-gallant sails flow out from the masts once more with that mysterious something which we call wind. Now our good ship seems to wake up, like one who has been taking a long nap, and hastens on her journey, to make up for lost time. We pass out by the Cape of Good Hope, though not in sight of it, into about fifty south latitude. Here we took the monsoon trade winds, which, as I said before, always blow west southerly, and some times blow very strong breezes. At any rate we found it so, for after squaring the yards and keeping our ship away before the wind, and setting our studding sails, we found our ship going through the water at the rate of eight or nine miles the hour; and this she averaged for more than thirty days, when we made the land, and were glad once more to see something besides our own solitary ship, which for months had been about all the world to us. This land proved to be the Island of Cracato, on the coast of Sumatra. Passing by this island, leaving it on the left, we soon made the Island of Java on the right hand, and entering in between

these two head lands we were now in the Straits of
Sunda, with Sumatra on the left and Java on the
right hand, the ship heading easterly. Passing one
hundred miles up the Straits of Sunda we found
ourselves in shoal water opposite the city of Batavia,
where we moored our ship, having accomplished the
passage in one hundred and twenty-seven days, from
Portsmouth, in England, to this land of spicy breezes.

Batavia is a Dutch colony, and is a place of much
trade. The land is very low and flat and the water
very bad, hence it is very sickly here, and many
European and American sailors have already laid their
bones here. Alligators abound here, also monkeys,
baboons, and jackalls. The bohunupas tree, it is said,
grows in this region, a tree so deadly poisonous that
no one can with safety approach within many rods of it.

Bank bills are worthless as shavings here; nothing
but the precious metals pass current in this city.
There are no wharves, and next kin to no tides. All
cargoes are brought along side in lighters. Our ship
received a cargo of sugar and coffee — sugar in bags,
six feet deep all over the lower hold, then mats all
over that, then came coffee in bags, till the lower hold
was filled. Between decks we had boxes of nut-
megs, and other merchandise in abundance, till this
large ship was filled fore and aft with a cargo worth
hundreds of thousands of dollars.

While lying here a Dutch fleet of men-of-war, consisting of three line-of-battle ships, came in and
anchored near us; one morning a silk handkerchief

was seen flying at our fore top gallant yard arm; this was a private signal for the admiral's ship's boat to come along side, which soon after took place; a boat with several men and officers came along side and the officers came on deck and enquired to know what was wanted. Several of our crew being Dutchmen wished to leave and go on board their own country's ships, notwithstanding they were men-of-war, rather than remain and be treated with so much severity as they were by the officers of our ship. This produced quite an altercation between the officers of the two ships, which resulted, however, in leaving our Dutchmen to remain where they were.

Our cargo now came alongside rapidly. A number of Malays were employed hoisting it on board, while we, the sailors, were fixing the rigging and preparing the ship for her homeward bound voyage. These Malays are a curious kind of people: two of them them would hoist about as much as one American. They eat little else but rice, and that about half boiled; this they eat invariably with the right hand, never using the left to put anything into their mouths. Spoons or knives they never to my knowledge make any use of in eating. They never sit on anything higher than that on which their feet rest — in fact, they seem to sit on their feet as near as I can come at it. Their clothing is a narrow strip of cotton (India to be sure) passed several times around the body and coming up between their legs and tying behind their backs, completely covering them from all indecent appearance to those who are familiar with their dress.

Their hair is the greatest curiosity about them; this is most commonly shaved or cut off except a patch about the size of a small plate; this, though reaching to their feet when strait, they contrive to form into a kind of mat which they place on the top of their head, which answers instead of a kind of scull cap. They never shave, but pull out their beard with tweezers, a little instrument kept handy for the purpose which they carry somehow about the waist.

Our cargo being about all on board, orders came from the captain on shore to bend the sails and get the ship ready for sea, all which was done with a hearty good will. Just as we were about to unmoor the ship, word came from the shore that our good friend the doctor, who went out as our physician, had died of the fever. These tidings were received with sadness, for he was a very nice gentleman and a good physician.

However, the captain, with all his movables, came on board the very next day, and we were once more under way, bound to Philadelphia, in the United States. Soon after leaving the Straits of Sunda a number of our crew were taken suddenly sick, one of which, the sailmaker, died in a very few days. His name was Daniel Sherman. Off the Cape of Good Hope we lost another man, by the name of Day; near the island of St. Helena, where Bonaparte was banished, we lost another of our crew; this was a Dutchman, aged about seventy years. He no doubt died of the hardship of the voyage. Cruel as our two mates were, they never sent this old sailor aloft, but the weather of the Cape of Good Hope was cold and boisterous, too much so for one of his years to stand the deck, especially in the night watches. These three we buried in the mighty deep.

Our passage home was long and tedious, partly on account of contrary winds, and partly on account of bad usage, a great scarcity of water, and want of sleep, never having our watch below except when it stormed so that we could do nothing on deck. Our water was all rain water caught in a building in the city built for that very purpose, and cost one dollar a cask when brought along side. It was good, but there was not enough of it, one quart, and even down to a pint and a half for twenty-four hours being for many weeks our daily allowance to a man. We had some terrible gales of wind between St. Helena and the West India Islands, spoke one ship bound to Africa and obtained from her several hogsheads of water. Soon after crossing the line we had a severe rain-storm, and by stopping the scuppers filled all our empty casks with water, so that we were allowed two quarts a day for the remainder of the voyage.

I have already hinted that we were not used well. So far as provisions were concerned we fared decently well, but our treatment as men or seamen was cruel; and to make this appear plain to the reader, I will here relate a circumstante which I think will place this matter before him in unmistakable plainness.

Since commencing to write this book, while overhauling some old letters, I most unexpectedly came across one that I wrote fifty-seven years ago to my parents in Castine, while in Batavia, on this very voyage, from which I will make an extract. "The usage on board this ship is very bad indeed. They have had much difficulty in retaining their men. Several of them left in Amsterdam, others in England, and while we are reefing the sails the first mate especially will spring aloft and on to the yards, and if these men, foreigners though they are, do not work to suit him, will beat one and kick another, so that the blood may, if ever we arrive in the United States, be seen on these topsails as witnesses against him." What if they were Dutchmen, they had rights that ought to have been respected, as well as any other men.

But they were Dutchmen and Swedes. Isaac Posin, the first mate, was a slaveholder, and liked the work of beating his brother man, and treating him as a brute, though possessed of a skin as white or whiter than his own. He was used to that sort of business—it had become a fixed habit with him. It was said by the second mate, I know not as to its truthfulness, that he had killed one man some years before with a handspike.

It may appear strange to the reader that the ship should pretend to be bound to Canton when in fact she was bound to Batavia; this I never knew the secret of, but I have thought that it might be to evade some clause in a treaty with the French or English, in order to avoid being made a prize of if overhauled by either of these two governments, as they were then at war with each other.

One day the captain told us we should see land in less than four hours. This proved true, for he was a skilful navigator (having been sailing master of a British man-of-war), and to our great joy in less than two hours "Land ho!" was cried out from the masthead, and sure enough there it was in plain sight. The main brace was immediately spliced; that is to say, all hands were called aft to take a drink of grog. New life seemed to enter into every one. We had been a long time at sea, and it was with sensations of joy that we once more beheld our own native shores of America.

A day or two after this we anchored off Newcastle, a handsome village on the southern shore of the river Delaware. Here in a little time both of our mates were missing, and on inquiry we were told that they had gone to Baltimore after money to pay us off with. The fact, however, proved to be that they, afraid of being arrested by some of the sailors they had abused on the voyage, had taken this course to escape the demands of justice. Here we lay several days without being permitted to go on shore, any of us except the boat's crew, of whom I happened to be one, for we all longed to be on terra firma once more. On the opposite shore of the river from the village from where our ship was moored we went on shore for fresh meat and vegetables, and such was the fear of the people that we were from some sickly port, and that they would take some disease, that it was with difficulty that we could approach near enough to a store there was there to let them know what we wanted. We, however, obtained what we wanted, and left the money where they directed and returned on board with a good supply of fresh beef and vegetables. A few days after we were called aft one at a time and paid off, all except enough to take care of the ship until a new crew could be obtained from Philadelphia.

On receiving my wages the captain wished to know if I would like to go to Amsterdam in the ship, that being the place where this valuable cargo was to be landed; I replied, " No sir, not with such usage as we have received during the late voyage to India." To which he immediately replied, " If my mates had not been smart to make the men do their duty, I would have driven them overboard themselves." This remark led me to suppose the mates not quite so much to blame as the old fellow himself was, he being a Scotchman, and formerly sailing master of an English man-of-war.

We were all landed at Newcastle, and forbidden to go up to the city short of forty days from the time we made the land, on the account of our having lost some men at sea with the fever. Little attention was paid to this, and we were soon in the then largest city in the Union. And thus ended one of the longest and hardest voyages of my life. And here let me say that I suffered more for the want of sleep than from any any other consideration whatever. Never allowed our watch below as I have already said, in the day time; and always every night obliged to be up four or eight hours, and never allowed below more than six one night and four the next alternately. Let any one try this for one year, and especially a youth, as I was, with no exception but the little time in port, and if they do not find themselves sometimes walking the deck in almost a profound sleep I should be greatly mistaken about human nature, and begin to think that I was different from most of the race in this respect. But we will say no more about this voyage at present, if we ever do.

CHAPTER III.

In the fall of 1804, having furnished myself with a good supply of clothes, and having attended school a few weeks, and having got rid of a considerable part of my money in various ways which it is no use here to mention, I began to think about taking another voyage to sea; and, having found a ship bound to the West Indies, I soon embarked on board the Concord, of Philadelphia, bound to Jamaica, thence to the Bay of Honduras, and thence to London. Captain George Davis, Master. Here I shipped for twenty-two dollars per month, having to find my own small stores, such as tea, coffee, sugar, and what other little nick nacks I had a mind to allow myself. This was a very large ship. We had a pleasant passage, a fatherly kind of a man for a captain, good officers, and a good crew of well trained seamen, most of whom knew their duty and did it cheerfully. Being about all of them Americans, there was peace and harmony among us.

We arrived in Jamaica all well, but got our ship on shore going up the harbor to Kingston, through some mismanagement of the pilot, which cost us a great deal of hard labor in carrying out anchors, heaving in cables, etc. By the help of other ship's crews who came to our assistance, we finally succeeded in getting the ship off, and got safe up to the city where we landed our cargo. Here at Port Royal lay several English men-of-mar, one of which was called the Thunderer, a French eighty-four gun-ship, which had been taken by the English and added to their navy. This ship had been out in a hurricane and got dismasted; and they were in want of men. Being on shore in the city one Sabbath, I was arrested by a press gang and shut up all night in one of the most filthy places imaginable, together with a number of others, without food or water or anything else until eight o'clock the next morning, when we were huddled into the boat and taken on board the above ship. The first thing that started me much was the unexpected discharge of a thirty-six pounder close by where I was standing. The next thing was the grum voice of the boatswain's mate ordering all the pressed men aft who had come on board that morning. Here was the old fellow himself, or rather I should have said the admiral, with his three cocked hat, dressed in his uniform — here were the lieutenants and other officers of the ship—here, too, was a band of martial music, bass and other drums, fifes and fiddles, clarionets and horns — everything that could give grandeur and interest to the scene. After the music ceased we were one by one ordered to our several stations on board the ship. Being a youth, I was sent into the fore top, where I fell in with a number of Americans, pressed men, who for years had been in His Majesty's service against their will.

Owing to the interposition of Divine Providence, as

I now think, I was spared the fearful doom of remaining long on board this floating mass of moral pollution and infamy. At about eleven we saw our own captain, Davis, come along side and on board the ship; he had our protections, and in the most dignified, decisive manner demanded our release from this ship, which after some altercation between him and the admiral, in which he was heard to say if his men were not immediately given up he should throw the ship on the admiral's hands, and write to the President the state of affairs at Jamaica. The admiral consented to let us go.

One hour's smart tugging of the boatmen at the oars, brought us once more to our own ship, at whose masthead the stars and stripes were floating in the gentle breeze. Never did they look more precious to us than at this moment. We felt as though we could cheerfully die in their defence. And even now, though past seventy-five and almost seventy-six, we feel no small degree of the same emotion.

Oh, how oft the very sight of these stars and stripes have caused the British lion to drop his tail and shrink away into some corner as though some awful castastrophe awaited him at their approach.

But to my story, a sad feature of which is now at hand; for in a day or two after this a youth by the name of Marshall, belonging in Philadelphia, only sixten, the youngest on board our ship, was suddenly struck down by the yellow fever, and died in about thirty-six hours. We buried him in the sand where the ship lay taking in ballast. Oh, how sad I felt at parting with that precious youth. The next one seized with this terrible disease was myself; then a young man by the name of Cook; now the doctor came on board and examined us, and as I was informed told the captain that my case was favorable, and he thought I should recover, but Cook he said must die, as his medicine could have but little power over the fever where the subject was habitually intemperate. And so it proved, for Cook was soon past all hope, and expired in awful agony. The fever continued to rage till every man before the mast had had it, sparing alive but seven of fourteen seamen, the most of whom were in the morning of their days.

After shipping some new hands, such as could be obtained, to make up the loss by the fever, we were soon on our way again bound to Balize, in the Bay of Honduras. Here we buried the last man who died with the fever; his name was Jack Hutten, and he was one of the best of seamen. Oh, how loth we were to give him up! but he must go; his fever turned to the black vomit, which soon terminated his earthly career. He died about nine in the evening, and was, like all the others, put into a coffin made of rough boards, placed in the long boat, and veered astern of the ship, where he remained till the next day, when he was taken on shore and buried. After this the ship was thoroughly cleaned, and no more sickness or death fell to our lot during our voyage.

In this place we took on board logwood and redwood enough to fill the fore peak and stern of the ship, and then because there was no mahogany there we had to go to a place called Golden River, on the Spanish Main, where the slaves had hewed and rolled out to the river a cargo of mahogany for us. While taking in this, we were made a prize of by His Majesty's ship-of-war Fly, Sir Edward Peliew's son being Commander. After loading our ship, which they wished us to do because it would increase the value of the prize if condemned, and if cleared we should be ready to proceed on our way to London, we were all taken on board the British man-of-war, and our ship was manned with a crew from the frigate. We now joined the fleet, consisting of thirty-three ships, all bound for England, loaded with dye-woods, mahogany, etc.

Nothing very alarming took place on our passage, except now and then a man would be brought to the gang-way and flogged for some misdemeanor or other, I could hardly ever learn what, except on one occasion, which I will here mention in order to give the reader some faint idea of British tyranny over poor helpless seamen in their navy. The man who kept the fowls by some accident or other let one of them escape from the hen-house, when it immediately flew overboard. For this carelessness, if carelessness it was, he was brought to the gang-way, lashed to a gun, and there on his naked back made to receive two dozen lashes with a cat-o-nine-tails, every blow of which made the blood fly, and caused this poor innocent victim to scream at the top of his voice with cries such as would pierce the heart unless terribly hardened in sin against God. We tacked ship off the Moro Castle at eight P. M., and at twelve the night following found ourselves on shore on a reef lying off Key Tabineer, on the Florida coast. The weather guns were then thrown overboard, a constant firing of the lee ones was kept up in order to alarm the fleet, which was a little astern of us, that they might tack ship and escape the danger, which they all did except the American ship out of which I was taken, and one other ship, belonging to London. These two were cast away close by, in sight of us.

Here we were, rolling and thumping fearfully. We soon cut away the jib boom and all three of the top masts, after which the ship lay quite still. Before daylight she had filled up to the mess deck. The carriage of a gun thrown from the main-top killed the sail-maker, who happened to be in the main rigging at the time — the gun itself having been lowered and thrown overboard a little before. At daylight we perceived that every ship had taken the alarm and tacked, and stood off shore, not one of them being in sight.

At break of day all hands were called aft to receive each one a glass of good West India rum. This seemed to warm us up, and we commenced getting the boats of the spar deck in readiness to embark for the land, it being about three miles under our lee. Soon, however, we discovered plenty of wrecking vessels in the harbor getting under way to come to our relief. Some of these were large schooners, which came as near us as they dared to, and anchored in the edge of the breakers, and by the help of boats succeeded in getting us all safe on shore except one poor old man who was very sick. What became of him I never knew.

Our water and provisions were now all submerged on board the frigate. We were on an uninhabited isle of the sea — about three hundred of us. We soon commenced digging wells, hoping to find water; but all in vain; no water except a very little the wreckers served out to us. Next day the sea became more smooth. Some of us returned on board the ship, and with plenty of negro divers, who went down under water into the hold of the ship, having a rope first made fast round one leg to haul them back by, when they should give the sign by kicking, we soon obtained bread, beef and pork plenty, with some other good things that sailors are apt to be fond of. But water was difficult to obtain; we notwithstanding made out to obtain enough to keep us from suffering.

We were wrecked on the fourth day of March, 1805, and it was an awful sight to see that great splendid ship rolling, tumbling, and surging in the breakers, her yards flying, masts bending, top-masts breaking, cannon roaring, and everything in a state of confusion. A man needed strong nerves in order to keep cool and collected in the midst of such a scene as this.

We were all busy for a day or two stripping the ship of her sails, and whatever could as well as not be saved from the wreck, after which she was set on fire and burned to the water's edge. It was said the object in burning was to prevent the enemy from getting anything out of her. It was a splendid sight to see her burn, and to hear the falling of cannon heated by the flames, hissing as they plunged into the gulf beneath.

After storing everything snugly on board the wreckers we made sail for Nassau, New Providence, where we arrived in a few days. Here I found myself about destitute of everything except what I stood in, and a little money for present emergencies, having lost chest and hammock on board the American ship out of which I was taken. Finding nothing better to do in this place, and no way to get to the United States, I entered on board of an English privateer schooner, called the Mayflower, Captain George Johnson, Master, for a six months' cruise. I received thirty dollars bounty money, and was to have so many shares of the prize money.

I had forgotten to say that the man-of-war and our ship Concord were bound to Jamaica to have her trial, when we were cast away. The trial, however, went on the same as though both ships had arrived safe, our ship was cleared, and the English government had to pay for both ship and cargo, and all other losses sustained on account of her capture. And here let me say, for the information of the reader, that our ship was taken because we took in sticks of mahogany larger than the treaty between the two governments admitted. But then we took it from Spanish territory, and that was why our ship was cleared in the Court of Admiralty, holden at Jamaica, where our ship was tried.

We now return to the privateer. This was the fastest sailing craft that ever I was in. I have known her to go through the water fourteen miles an hour, with a taught bowline. We had on board seventy-five men, all told. Sixty of those were slaves, and belonged mostly to the captain. The remainder were white men, officers, etc. We had two double-fortified long twelve-pounders on pivots, and a brass six-pounder on the forecastle, together with about fifty stand of small arms, to be used by the marines; also boarding-pikes, hatchets, and other implements of death, to be used as best they could be in case of an engagement with the enemy. We were well prepared to cope with any craft of our size. And though most of our men were slaves, they were nevertheless smart and active as any of the *Anglo Saxon* race. The gunner and boatswain were both as black as Chloe, but aside from this they were handsome featured and well-built men about as I ever saw, and understood their duty as well as any other men in His Majesty's service.

The English were now at war with the French and Spanish. We took many prizes, though mostly under the American colors, some of which were cleared, being found to be American property, and some of which were condemned, being found to be French or Spanish property.

We used often to go on shore on the Island of Cuba, and plunder the inhabitants by shooting down some of their cattle, so as to keep ourselves well stocked with fresh beef, vegetables, etc., etc. Once we run in between two forts, where their cannon could not be brought to bear upon us, into a narrow place where there was a little village, where we frightened the inhabitants so it was absolutely amusing to see the men, women, and children running in every direction through fear of being hurt by us, who had no more disposition to harm them than we had to harm ourselves. One of their head men, accompanied by others, came down on the quay where our schooner was lying, with a paper in his hand written by an English captain of a man-of-war, forbidding any of His Majesty's subjects to molest in any way whatever these innocent, unoffending citizens, they having been very kind to some unfortunate British seamen who had been cast away near there some years before. We traded with them what we wished to, and then made sail and returned from between these two forts, though not without receiving a number of shots from the enemy.

At another time we were sailing down along shore, perhaps twenty or thirty miles south-west of Havana, and being almost out of fresh meat, some half-dozen of us were sent on shore with muskets and knives, to take whatever came to hand. Going up the bank into a pasture we observed a herd of cattle, among which was a fat heifer. This we singled out and put two or three balls through the head at once, bringing her to the ground. We off head and out entrails, and without stopping to take off the hide we cut her into four pieces and started for the boat. Just as we had got seated at our oars, whiz! whiz! came the bullets from behind a bunch of bushes. This only made us pull a little harder, while those not rowing returned the compliment with some considerable derterity, without, I should think, harming any one.

At another time we were off Havana just at night, when we discovered a Spanish schooner at the mouth of the harbor. Preparations were now made for cutting her out, as it is called. This is done by sending in boats, well manned and armed, for the purpose of cutting the cable and getting the vessel under way, after fastening the men below. As soon as night came on volunteers were called for, to man the boats to go in and bring out the anticipated prize; but on going into the mouth of the harbor, we found her laying a little too near the fort for our safety, hence we with muffled oars returned without our intended prize.

At a certain time we had been laying too most of the night in thick weather, without knowing precisely where we were, but as the day dawned we found ourselves rather nearer the Moro Castle than was desirable. We softly called all hands, and commenced with oars muffled to pull our vessel out of the reach of their shot; but before this could be done we saw the fiery flashes of their guns, and soon the whistling balls came hissing by us, sometimes cutting off the oars with which we were pulling ourselves out of danger. Having about a dozen oars on each side of our fast sailing schooner, we could row her with ease four miles an hour when there was no wind, as was the case at this time, consequently we were soon out of the reach of our enemy.

Off Havana at another time one morning we discovered a large schooner, with Spanish colors flying at the mast head, making for the harbor with all possible speed. We immediately gave chase, and clearing away our bow chaser, we gave them round shot till we came quite near them. At last they hove too and hauled down their colors, and we made a prize of them. It proved to be a Spanish King's packet, from New Orleans, bound to Havana. We landed her men near Havana, and sent the prize into Nassau, New Providence.

After this we changed our cruising ground, and in company with another small privateer belonging to our captain, we went to the mouth of the Mississippi to try our luck in that vicinity. Here we fell in with a schooner under American colors, which we captured on suspicion of her being French property. How this was I know not, but one thing I do know, and that is, we were glad to give her up. How it was I know not, but somehow or other the captain of the American cutter laying at Beleze, a distance up the river, got tidings of the affair, and came down and began to pepper us with shot, so that we were glad to get our men out of the expected prize again, and make off with ourselves as fast as possible. Here were two English privateers against one American cutter, and both of them scampering for life to get out of the way of Uncle Sam's round shot, and I was inwardly laughing about it all the while, hoping they would make a prize of us, so I could get clear of them, for I was quite disgusted with the business of privateering, and had already made up my mind to escape the first opportunity.

On our way back to the coast of Florida we fell in with and captured a French privateer. This was the first and only fair battle that I was ever in on the high seas. This lasted about an hour, when victory turned on our side, and we boarded the enemy and drove them all below except the wounded who were lying on the deck. We then fixed a plank from one vessel to the other, and those poor souls were made to walk on board our vessel and go below, where they were all put in irons for safe keeping till we should have an opportunity to set them on shore or send them home as prisoners of war.

In this battle there was some blood spilt. One of our men was blown up some ten or a dozen feet high by the premature explosion of a cartridge he was ramming down at the time. Our gun-smith received a ball through the hip which disabled him forever. But the most appaling sight was the wounded prisoners.

One had a grape shot directly through the palm, taking away the most of his hand; another had a bullet pass through his breast; some were wounded in the legs so they could not stand. It was an awful sight — such as I never desire to witness again, either in this world or in that which is to come. We did the best we could for the comfort of the wounded prisoners till they were sent to the hospital; how it fared with them after that I never knew.

We lay most of one night with our matches lighted and burning, expecting every moment to be fired into from a vessel we had seen just at dusk the evening before. Owing to thick weather this vessel loomed up and appeared to be of some account; but what was our chagrin, when in the morning we discovered it to be nothing but a small fishing smack which we had been standing in such fear of during the night.

A privateersman's life is of all occupations the most wretched. If I must go into this kind of business, let me go on board a first rate line-of-battle ship; then there is no fear of any one ship, let it be what it may. Not so with the privateer; every thing alarms, and we are always fearing a superior force.

After being in this miserable business about two months, I was sent in prize-master of a Spanish schooner we had captured, merely to clear some point in the law, because it was contrary to law for a colored man to have charge of any vessel of war in those days, so that I merely answered as a substitute for a prize-master. Having arrived safe in port with our prize, and having to wait here till the Mayflower should come in, I took it into my head to look for some other employ.

I soon found a vessel — one of those very ones that we had shortly before taken — having been bought by a French gentleman, who wanted to ship hands for New Orleans. Accordingly I sold my prize money for just what I could get, to a merchant in Nassau, giving him a power of attorney so that it became his. I bade adieu to privateering, and embarked on board this craft, to go first to Exumar, take in a cargo of salt, thence to Havana, in Cuba, and then, under American colors, to go to New Orleans. When I first went on board this vessel I saw in the cabin with the captain a youth, who he informed me was his son. This I never called in question on our voyage to Havana. Went to Exumar, one of the Bahama Islands, took in our cargo of salt, and then was windbound a number of days, during which time we lived mostly on what is called conks — there being no inhabitants on this island, we could get no supplies of provisions. We at last got out of this lonely place and got to another island, where there was a wealthy slaveholder living, where we got some corn, which we had to grind ourselves in order to have some bread. This we did with two stones about the size of common grind stones, the upper one of which we whirled round by means of a stick inserted in it near the edge. Having ground our corn and got some other provisions, we went on board and got under way once more, heading for Havana. On our passage thither we had moderate weather and smooth sea, except we had to reef topsails once, in doing which, as I passed out on the yard-arm, I accidently knocked a Spaniard's hat off his head, which had a considerable quantity of cut tobacco and paper, all ready for making cigars, after their fashion. This all went overboard together, which so enraged the man that after our sails were reefed and he had liberty to go below, I saw him sharpening his knife, which another Spaniard who could speak a little English told me to beware of, as he had no doubt he intended to be avenged on me for the loss of his hat, etc. This alarmed me some, knowing the revengeful disposition of the Spaniard. For several nights when it was my watch below, I used to lie down on deck near the wheel, where the man at the helm could arouse me if he saw danger approaching. We soon after this arrived in Havana, and there became friendly to each other. Still I had no inkling to sail with Spaniards, especially as we had a Frenchman for our captain, none of them being able to understand me or I them very well. Instead of the captain's son, a young lady came on deck and went on shore in the boat with the captain. Once after this, one afternoon, she came off in a boat, with a view to come on board, which the captain with some very hard words prevented, so with the boatman she returned with her eyes full of tears. That was the last I ever saw or heard of her. Shortly after this a sailor belonging to a Boston ship, one night, in attempting to go on board his vessel, fell overboard and was drowned. Hearing of this, I concluded if the captain desired it to take his place, which I accordingly did, and was soon on my way to Boston. We had a good passage home, and I found it very pleasant to be among my own countrymen once more.

After arriving in Boston, and seeing some of my old acquaintances, and especially my old friend Waters, the printer, whom I found here, I began to think about going back to Philadelphia to get my wages for services rendered on board the ship Concord, previous to her being cast away on the coast of Florida, as I have before stated. Having found a packet sloop bound directly there, I put my things on board ready for a start the first wind. Capt. Constant Norton, a distant relative, commanded this vessel, and had been in this business for years. Providence, however, seemed to order it so that I should not go to Philadelphia just now, for, falling in with a brother-in-law of mine in the street, he insisted so hard on my going home to see my friends, and withal telling me how overjoyed my poor mother would be to see me, that I finally yielded, and consented to let the wages go for the present, and so took passage with him and went home to Castine to my friends and parents, in the fall of 1805, after an absence from them of about three years and a half, they having never heard from me during all that time but twice, and I having never heard from them at all.

My return was not precisely like that of the prodigal's, because I was well clothed, etc., but I carried nothing away with me and returned with but little, having been cast away and repeatedly robbed of part of what I had, by land sharks and others, who stand ready to take every possible advantage of the inexperienced and uninstructed. There was joy, however, in my father's house; they were glad that one of their number who had been so long absent, and who they had but very little expectation of ever seeing again, had returned safe and sound.

After visiting old friends and acquaintances for some few weeks, I once more entered the district school for a season, where I made good progress in my studies, seeing that we had an able teacher. After being at home some months and the school having closed, and after doing up some work for my father, I began to feel like taking another voyage to sea. Accordingly I shipped on board the ship Ruthy, of Lincolnville, bound to Havana, a vessel commanded by Capt. Samuel Bullock, my brother, Phineas Norton, being first mate. When about to sail I took good care and sent my father some money, to remunerate him for board while going to school.

January 1806. We are now on our way to the West Indies, and the vapor is so thick, the weather being exceedingly cold, that it is difficult finding our way down the Penobscot Bay; we, however, got to sea without much difficulty, and in a few days across the gulf, where the water is so warm that we choose to go barefooted except when we go aloft. We experienced nothing remarkable on the outward bound passage except that the weather was so fine and so moderate that we had no occasion to reef a topsail or furl a top gallant sail. One catastrophe we experienced which I ought to name; it may serve as a caution to some one who may chance to read this book. In passing over the Bahama Banks by steering too southerly a course we got into shoal water, where our ship found. herself unable to proceed further without being lightened of a part of the cargo, which was thrown overboard and lost. And after carrying out anchors and heaving in cables for some twenty four hours, we finally succeeded in getting into deeper water, and so proceeded on our voyage, without any farther annoyance till we arrived safe in Havana. We went up to a place called the Regulars, where we discharged our cargo, which consisted of pine boards to make sugar boxes. These boards some of them had ice on them so thick that it remained on them till the negroes took hold of them to draw them out of the water, they being carried on shore in large rafts; these darkies, when they felt the cold ice as they took them under their arms, would cry out most piteously, not knowing what it meant, having never handled any ice before.

The Havana is a very sickly port indeed, but we were all blest with good health during the entire voyage. I have heard it said that there are as many cannon mounted here in and about this harbor as there are days in a year.

We took in a cargo of molasses and sugar and

started for Castine, at which place we arrived after a stormy passage of about forty days.

My venture consisted of a barrel of honey, which turned very well in Castine, being purchased by the same good doctor who doctored and cured my foot so many years before.

After remaining on shore a short time, and enjoying social intercourse with friends and neighbors, I took another voyage to sea in the brig Vigilant, belonging to James Crawford, Esq., of Castine. This was a good vessel excepting one fault she had, that she was one-sided; not in the same way that some people are in regard to politics, but this vessel was made so from the beginning. She was built so. One bow was much fuller than the other, — one man timbered out one bow and went away, and another came and timbered out the other, hence the difference. On one tack she would lay to most completely, but on the other not at all.

We arrived in Liverpool after an excellent passage of only twenty-five days, during which a common yawl boat would have been perfectly safe, so far as wind or sea was concerned. In Liverpool I fell in with some of the crew of the ship Concord, about which I have had occasion to say so much; they asked me if I had been to Philadelphia after my wages. I said no. They said they had, and were honorably paid off; that they had no doubt but that I should be, if I would take the trouble to go. I told them I thought I should when I had leisure. But more of this hereafter. Here we boarded on shore, not (as I have already observed) being allowed the use of fire on board the vessel except in a safe lantern with water in the bottom of it. We fared well here, having plenty to eat and drink of that which was good and wholesome.

Here again I saw an old sea captain, with whom I had had such a time some years before on our way to New York. Now the boot was on the other leg. From being a boy I had become a man; he had gained nothing, I had gained much, to say the least, in physical force, and when I met him on the quay one disrespectful look of the eye, one unpleasant word from his lips, and he would have found himself assuming a horizontal position a little sooner than he would have cared to.

Our cargo of lumber was soon out, and we again took freight for Castine. On our homeward bound passage off the Western Islands we encountered what is sometimes termed a white squal, such a one as none of us had ever seen before.

We were standing along with a moderate breeze from the southeast, our top gallant sails furled, all other sails set, heading about west southwest; at eight A. M. the wind began to veer to the south and west, with drizzly rain. I had the care of the captain's watch on deck, and happened at that moment to be at the helm myself. The wind still heading off, I kept the helm hard up to make the brig fall off before the wind. Being loaded with salt, she was amazing stiff.

All at once I felt her settling on to one side, no wind scarcely to be felt on deck; yet I perceived the topmasts were bending and the sails appeared to be full; in a moment the brig righted and everything remained as before. I thought it was nothing but a kind of a gust of wind, still I observed we were shooting ahead rapidly; helm hard up, brig terrible unwilling to fall off, though she did just about as fast as the wind slewed. All at once she took another lurch and settled rapidly on to one side. All hands were on deck as quick as possible, and notwithstanding every topsail sheet was either cut or let go instantly, trysail hauled down, staysail sheets cast off, and nothing left to hold any wind but the foresail. Such was the violence of the squal that we came very near running under water.

What of our sails did not get blown away we furled as well as we could, and then scud under the goose-wings of our foresail for about four hours, and then hove to under a balanced reefed trysail with our full bow to the leeward, which caused our vessel to lay to, and head the wind so completely that scarcely any spray flew over us, although the sea soon commenced running almost mountains high.

In due time we arrived safe in Castine, discharged our cargo, received our wages, and each one went their own way.

In the fall of 1806 I took another voyage to the West Indies in the schooner Mary, of Castine, Ebenezer Perkins, Master, myself for the first time mate. This was the first voyage my brother Noah, next younger than I, who afterwards became a Baptist minister of the gospel, ever went to sea. We went to Antigua, where we landed our cargo, which sold for twenty-eight dollars per thousand, cash, and took in ballast and returned home.

This would have been a very good voyage for the owners had it not been for a misfortune which befel us on the passage home. We were just thirteen days from Antigua, when we discovered the chain of mountains on the island of Mount Desert. This was the first day of February, 1807; the weather was extremely could, so that a man could not stand at the helm but about half an hour before his face would commence freezing, and he would have to be relieved by another. The wind now coming in shore and blowing about three days an incessant gale, we were blown back again almost into warm weather, — at any rate we got rid of all our ice, for we were badly iced up when we made the land. Now to make this story short as possible, lest I trespass on the reader, I will only observe that we were blown off three times and as often blown on again before we got safe into port. We were the whole month of February driving off and on the coast without any possibility of safely making the land after we made it the first time, on account of the extreme thickness of the weather every time the wind would become fair.

During this time the weather became so cold that the frost, as we supposed, getting into our chain bolts, they every one on the starboard side forward gave way at once, and away went our foremast, rigging, sails, and all, over the lee bow into the sea, leaving us a mere wreck to do the best we could with our square sail boom for a jury foremast. Having lost most of our sails, we could do but little at beating to windward; hence our voyage home was very much protracted. We were at length driven into Penobscot Bay in a severe rain storm, not knowing exactly where we were till we found ourselves in smooth water, under the lee of Owl's Head Island.

We now made ready to anchor, being resolved not to be blown off again very soon. In about three hours from this, the wind having changed again and come round northwest, seemed determined to drive us out to sea again, but we were a little too near home for it this time; and at eight o'clock P. M., on the first day of March, 1807, it being the Lord's day, we plumped her on shore, and making fast to the wharf furled our sails as well as we could, seeing they were already frozen almost as stiff as leather, and went up to the owner's house, which was merely to let them know that we had arrived safe, notwithstanding the fearful storm that had been raging all that day.

The people could hardly imagine how it was possible for a vessel to come in from sea the way we did, with our helm a lee and the vessel drifting at the mercy of the winds and waves, among rocks and ledges where no vessel ever attempted to pass, in the best of weather, with a fair wind; but Divine Providence interposed, heard prayer, for there were prayers put up to God for us that day. There being a religious meeting at my father's house, — as I have before stated, it being the Sabbath day, — the ministers, for there were two of them, students of the Rev. Daniel Merrill, of Sedgwick, were by my parents requested to remember their two sons at sea, which these faithful servants of the Lord accordingly did, and prayed so earnestly to God for us that the people took special notice of it and spoke of it as remarkable after the meeting closed. While we were tossing, plunging and rolling on the restless waves, near the ragged rocks, that unseen Power, who holds the winds in his fists, heard and answered prayer in our behalf, and brought us safe to the desired haven, where we, after enduring so much suffering, desired to be.

Bear with me, kind reader, while I give vent to my feelings by inserting one verse of Dr. Watts beautiful poetry, composed from the one hundred and seventh Psalm, which reads thus:

> 'T is God that brings them safe to land;
> Let stupid mortals know
> That waves are under his command,
> And all the winds that blow.

Here I wish to say, if you are a parent, take encouragement from this remarkable interposition of Divine Providence in answer to prayer, not only to pray for your children at sea, if such you have, but also to ask others, and most certainly ministers, to pray for them. Also, I would here say to Ministers, pray for the adventurous sailor; God will hear and answer prayer.

What renders the above circumstance still more worthy of special notice is the interesting fact, that both myself and my brother, who was younger than I, afterwards became ministers of the gospel, and preached the gospel in that same house where a few years before such fervent prayers had been offered up to God in our behalf.

In the spring of 1807, business being rather dull at Castine, I took a passage to Boston, and shipped on board the good ship Algol as Second Mate, to go to Bordeaux, in France. Thomas Follansbee commanded this ship, and a worthy man he was too. We had a very pleasant voyage indeed, no event taking place whatever that I can now call to mind, worthy a place in this little book, except we came near losing our cook, who was a colored man, and rather fond of strong drink. One afternoon not being very busy we took it into our heads to strip and jump overboard and see who was the best swimmer amongst us. Cuffee seeing this thought he would share in the sport, when off goes his duds and in he comes among us, black as ink and spouting like a porpoise. Having noticed that he rather tumbled than jumped overboard, I felt little suspicious of him, knowing that there was plenty of brandy below, where he could get at it if so minded, I kept an eye out for him to see how he succeeded in swimming. Shortly I perceived him sink out of sight, then he came up again spouting and shaking his head, not moving about much in any direction, all which increased my suspicions that he needed looking after; accordingly I swam towards him and found him already so exhausted, and withal so full of water, as to be unable to answer when spoken to. Immediately I called for help, which came as quick as possible, but a moment later and he would have sunk to rise no more to consciousness, till the judgment of the great day. A rope, however, from the ship's bows made fast around him, well manned by those who remained on deck, soon brought darkey on board, and put an end to our sport for that day.

Our cargo home consisted principally of wine and brandy. We had a pleasant passage, and arrived all well in the city of Salem, a little before the great embargo of 1807.

Here in Salem I shipped on board a fine new ship, to go to Calcutta, as chief mate, and got the ship ready for sea. It was said about this time that William Gray had already hauled up fifteen of his best ships. How that was I know not, but one thing was certain, it looked very squally between the governments of Great Britain and the United States; so much so that our owners, Captain Blunt and others, concluded not to send this ship to sea for the present. They finally sold the ship and bought a brig, and put me on board of her to get her ready for sea, which thing I accordingly did. We were to sail the next day, when the afternoon previous the captain, John Perkins, of Kennebunk, came on board and said the brig was likewise sold.

I then thought it would be as well for me to give it up for the present, and go home to Castine and see my folks once more, and spend the winter among my friends. Accordingly I took passage on a coaster bound to Eden by way of Belfast, where we had to stop to land some goods for the Honorable Judge Read, who was then about moving into the County of Waldo, together with some three hundred apple trees. On our passage down east we put into Portland for a harbor, and anchored in what is called Hog Island Roads. Here we rode out a severe gale, which came near driving us on shore, and probably would, had we not sent down our yards and launched our top masts, a job seldom done by coasters whether they go ashore or not. After the gale was over we got our yards aloft and top-masts up, and got under way, reaching Belfast next day. Here we discharged the freight and the trees, which I may have occasion to speak of again before I get through with this history of my life. We now made sail and cast off from the wharf, bound for Eden. When abreast of my father's house, in Brooksville, the schooner was hove too, the boat hauled up, and I, together with my chests, trunks, etc., landed in what is called Buck's Harbor. This was just after daylight, and as the sun was about rising I entered my father's house once more, having been from home about seven or eight months.

My folks, of course, were glad to see me, and I as

glad to see them. An old lady living in the street where I boarded in Salem, told me in fun one day, after she found out that I was going home, that the first female I should see after arriving home would finally become my wife. Singular as this may appear, it so turned out. My mother having during the summer taken a tour to Martha's Vineyard, took home with her a niece, a cousin of mine, to live with her a short season. Just as I entered the house, my father meeting me at the door, and while shaking hands with me, another front room door opened gently, and out stepped a beautiful young lady, not quite eighteen years of age, who on the thirtieth day of March following became my affectionate wife.

As I have already said, on the twenty-second day of December, 1807, the Embargo Bill passed both Houses of Congress and became a law, stopping all vessels at home and putting an end to foreign trade for the present.

The winter of 1808 passed pleasantly away with me, of course. I tried to improve my time, however, as well as I could, helping my father some about his work, studying some, preparing myself for any business I might find to do. In the course of the winter I hired with my brother who paid the printer for my time, and paid him up what remained due.

As I remarked before, on the thirtieth day of March, 1808, after mature deliberation on the subject, I took to myself a companion for life — a young lady by the name of Polly Norton, who had been brought up by a pious grandmother, in the town of Tisbury, Dukes County, Massachusetts, with whom I lived forty years, lacking a few days, in all the mutual and dear relations of husband and wife.

After taking a trip to Boston with my wife, in order to accompany her on the way to visit her friends, I returned and spent the summer about home. I finally engaged to mow a man's field for him, which I found rather an uphill business, as I had never been accustomed to swinging the scythe. I got through with it, however, in good season, though it proved rather an unprofitable job.

About the middle of August my wife returned from Massachusetts, and we commenced house-keeping. I remained at home all the following winter and spring. The Embargo Law, which still remained in force to some extent, was at this time so modified that vessels could go to England. Consequently the new ship Thucydidies, which had been built during the embargo, was immediately fitted for sea, and my brother and myself were engaged by the owner, Mr. Crawford, to go out in her as first and second officers.

My brother's health was very poor, being troubled with a distressing cough, so that he went the voyage perhaps as much to try to find help, as for any thing else; and in this he succeeded in some measure, for he was much better when we left Liverpool than when we arrived there, though not entirely well. Our voyage in this new ship was laborious though prosperous, and we accomplished it in about six months. On our passage out, on the Grand Banks we fell in with many icebergs, some of which we narrowly escaped. We had some heavy gales to encounter, but our new ship performed admirably, being perfectly tight and an excellent sea boat. In discharging our cargo in Liverpool we had some difficulty; the timber having been all winter in the ship's hold, had so swollen as to more than fill the port out of which it had to pass, and notwithstanding the great strength of those English horses which drew it forth out of the ship, it sometimes rubbed so hard against the sides of the port it was with difficulty they could start it more than a few inches at a pull. We took in a cargo of salt for Boston, at which place we arrived some time in the fall of 1809. In the spring of 1810 we again sailed for Liverpool, in the same ship and in the same capacity as before. This time we had contrary winds and very rough weather, which caused our passage to be somewhat lengthy, and made it very hard for my brother, who stood his watch till we made the land, when he gave out, and never did any more duty on shipboard. On our arrival in port, he stepped into a carriage and was conveyed to the house of the same doctor who had attended him when there the year before, but failed fast. His cough became more and more distressing, so that it was evident he could not hold out a great while longer.

Our ship being nearly ready for sea, and having shipped a second mate to fill my place, while I had to take my brother's place, I asked him one day if he thought of returning in the ship with us, or to stay and come home in some other ship, after getting better, if he ever should. To which he replied, that if he could live to get home, he should rather return in the ship; and in order to settle this point as near as possible, he wished me to ask the opinion of some skillful physician, which I accordingly did. Doctor McCurdy, one of the most skillful physicians in Liverpool, after a thorough examination into his case, gave it as his opinion that he would not survive over twenty days, though he said he thought he might possibly live fifty days. He then gave me a memorandum of what he thought best for him to eat and drink, etc., on the way home, provided he should conclude to take passage with us, all which was provided for him before leaving port. On informing him of the doctor's opinion concerning his living to return home, he wished to know how long I thought it would take to make the passage. I said about forty days. After thinking a few minutes, he calmly said: "You will make the necessary provisions, and I shall endeavor to return home with you. I'd rather die with you than die with strangers, and possibly I may live to return once more; if not, the will of the Lord be done." All this was said with so much calm resignation, that I could but weep at the thought of losing that dear brother. A day or two after this interview he was conveyed in a covered carriage to the place where the boat lay ready to receive him, and put carefully on board the ship. He was able to walk about the deck a little when he first came on board, though he seemed to take very little notice of what was going on. As soon as we got to sea he took to his room, and never came on deck any more till he had passed over the Jordan of death to a mansion above, that I believe Christ had prepared for him. Soon after he was taken on board, the ship was got under way and hastened on her voyage across the broad Atlantic. The steward of the ship was told by the captain to give his whole time, if needed, to the care of Mr. Norton, so that he was as well provided for as circumstances would allow on shipboard. He lived just twenty-two days after coming on board the ship. At five o'clock A. M. on the twentieth of August, 1810, he departed this life, in the morning of manhood, aged thirty years, two months, and fifteen days. He was the oldest of seven sons, and certain it is that he was one of the best of them, if there was any difference in them. He was especially endeared to me, not only because he was a brother, but because he was an affectionate brother. This appears at once when we consider what he did for me in advancing the money necessary to clear me from the demands of the printer. I have often thought it a striking incident of Divine Providence, that I should have the privilege of being with him in his sickness, and in his last moments. But he has gone, to return no more till the sea shall give up the dead that are in it. The day after his decease the ship was hove too for several hours, the American ensign was hoisted at the mizzen peak, the afteryards were thrown aback, the weather being fine and the sea smooth, the ship lay as still as though she knew her first officer was about to be buried in the bosom of the great deep. Everything being ready, the new canvas sack containing the body, with sufficient weights attached to it to cause it gently to sink to the bottom, was laid upon a plank prepared for the purpose and carefully lowered down the ship's side, and canted over so that the corpse was left to settle away gradually from our view, to be seen no more till the dead, small and great, shall stand before that tribunal to which all must come to give an account of the things done in the body, whether they be good or whether they be evil.

This was a solemn scene to me, never to be erased from my memory while I am capable of remembering anything. Oh! how solemn that afternoon — that evening, and how lonely that quarter deck. And even now, after the lapse of fifty-one years, the events of that day and that night are as vivid in my memory as though they had taken place but a few days ago.

We arrived in Boston, discharged most of our cargo, and then returned to Castine. Going into the harbor our colors were all set half-mast high, out of respect to him we had left in the bosom of the deep. Many a heart was sad that day, especially the bereaved widow, who could scarcely endure the thought of seeing us all return safe and sound but the one above all others that was dear to her heart.

CHAPTER IV.

Our good ship was once more loaded and made ready for sea, to carry out another cargo of pine lumber to Old England, for the use of that country, where boards enough to make a coffin will cost you about three guineas, or say, twelve dollars. We now have a new crew and a new second mate, who is my brother younger than I.

Our owner wanted to send the ship out in the winter, lumber at the time being very high, and worth more than usual.

The first or second day of January, 1811, we sailed from Castine with a fair wind, and after riding out a severe snow storm in Owl's-head harbor, so called, we again weighed and sailed for Europe. This proved to be a terrible cold and stormy passage. We experienced some severe gales, though our ship made no complaint, but proved herself fully equal to the conflict, being well manned and well managed.

Nothing alarming took place till after we made the land, when sailing up St. George's Channel we made a very small mistake; and in consequence of steering a little too much to the north of east, we had to pass in shore, or to the northward, of the Tuscar Rock, which is a very small island, inshore of which no large vessel ever attempts to pass unless driven to through sheer necessity. This brought us considerably to leeward of our course, and finally ended in the loss of our ship, and well nigh in the loss of all our lives, as the sequel will show.

The wind being southeasterly and blowing a gale, we could never make up that loss; that is to say, we could never get so far to windward as we needed to be on our direct course from Cape Clear to Holy-head. The wind increasing and heading us off, we soon found ourselves nearing the Irish coast, but made out to fetch along shore up the Channel that night till the next morning, when we discovered the land not more than four or five miles under our lee bow. The wind having become fixed, and blowing a gale, we might, and ought to, have gone into Waterford, which was under our lee. But no; our captain was a little too stout for that, and on we sped our way, other vessels all making a harbor as fast as possible. We however continued on, carying sail at a fearful rate, the sea breaking over us in a manner almost alarming.

One of two things now must be done. We had already passed by a good harbor, and there was none ahead that we could possibly reach as the wind then was, consequently we must either lighten the ship or shorten sail. If we shortened sail, the ship would inevitably go on shore where we must all hands have perished in the breakers. Accordingly we concluded to lighten the ship of all the lumber, spars, etc., that was on the upper deck.

This being done, our ship seemed to make rather better weather for a time. But alas! the gale increased to a fury, so that we must now reef or carry our masts over the side. With much difficulty a reef was taken in each top-sail, and all the stay-sails furled but the storm stay-sails. This seemed to relieve the ship a little, though she would plunge fearfully into the sea at times, which was now running mountain high and breaking on the shore to the leeward of us with awful grandeur.

In an hour or so after reefing, we discovered breakers very near us under the lee bow, to avoid which we concluded to try our ground tackling. The topsails, fore and aft, were immediately furled, everything made as snug as possible, and the helm put hard a lee, and the ship brought head to the wind under her storm mizzen, and the best bower anchor let go. Here we were, near the foaming, thundering billows, our beautiful ship laboring, rolling, and plunging, as if anxious to be cut loose from this terrible condition. The sea proved to be too strong for our anchor, ponderous as it was, and though it held on marvelously for a short time, the wind and sea both increasing in power and force, our noble ship began to drift and bring (as sailors call it) the anchor home.

Now came another dilemma. The cable must be cut, the ship got under way and steered clear of these breakers, or immediate death was our inevitable lot.

In this critical moment a consultation was had, when it was agreed unanimously to cut the cable, run up the head-sails, and if possible pass to windward of these breakers, and prepare to run the ship on shore, as we had now lost all hope of keeping her off till the gale should abate so that we could carry sail again. We accordingly cut the cable, run up the fore top-mast stay-sail, and just escaped those sunken ledges which would have broken our ship to pieces in a very few moments had she have been made of steel. Here I, though a poor ignorant sinner, could but see the hand of God in our escape from this fearful dilemma. We were now about one mile from the shore, drifting rapidly toward the breakers. The captain and myself now went on to the fore yard to see if we could discover some place where the ship could be run on shore with some prospect of saving our lives. In this we were fortunate enough to see a place where we thought she might be run so near the shore without striking as to render it possible for us to escape some how or other. When directly abreast of this chosen spot of life or death, the helm was put hard up, the ship fell off before the sea, and in another moment, as it were, she was flying upon the top of a mighty wave, which carried her so far on shore that when that wave left her it was as if she had been let fall from some twenty feet in the air, striking with such a fearful crash, and so sudden, that it brought every man flat to the deck — he could not tell how, only each man found himself prostrated. In this fearful moment every man had to look out for himself. Two men at the helm were admonished to stand away from it; this and the cry: "Let every man take care of himself!" were the last orders given on

this occasion, except to tell them not to hold on to
cleats or belaying pins, but to lay hold on the shrouds
when the next sea came. Here we were, flat on the
land, another sea approaching with awful fury, came
tumbling over us, burying us far beneath its foaming
surface, overwhelming our ship as it passed, though
not without carrying us some distance towards terra
firma, to which all seemed just now in want to gain,
having drank quite salt water enough for the present.
It was curious to notice what the second sea did to us
after the ship struck. It whirled the ship entirely
round, causing her to lay broad side to the sea, broke
the rudder in three pieces, stove the stern boat entirely to pieces, and broke some three or four of the
main deck beams, etc., etc. The sea continued to
break all over us perhaps ten or fifteen feet high, all
hands taking care of themselves as best they could.

A thought struck my mind just at this juncture of
affairs, to make fast a rope to a plank that I had saved
when cleaning the deck in the morning, and let the
sea take it on shore. This was accordingly done, and
just at that moment two Irishmen came to the spot,
saw and secured the plank, holding on to the end of
the rope. The captain, who now stood in the gang-
way, seeing what was done, says: "I will go on shore,
Mr. Norton." "Very good," said I, "step on deck
and I will make this rope fast around you," which I
accordingly did, taking care at the same time to make
the deep-sea line fast to the rope to haul it back by.
The two men on the shore, perceiving what was doing

on board the ship, prepared themselves for the struggle, and as soon as they saw the captain jump overboard they commenced hauling for life, to save life, but it was a narrow escape. The captain was a very heavy man, being six feet and three inches in his stockings, and withal rather fleshy, and having in his haste leaped into the sea when the sea was down, it gave the two men a terrible tug to pull him on shore, being some ten or fifteen feet under water, on account of the sea that overwhelmed him immediately after leaving the ship. They succeeded, however, in getting him out of the surf, although it was some time before he could stand.

Seeing him safe on shore, I immediately drew back the rope, which the captain, who had now so far recovered from his perilous condition as to take good care of the end of, so that we should not lose our means of conveyance from the ship to the shore.

The next sent on shore was the second mate, who, while clearing the decks in the morning, had some how got his ankle hurt so that he was about disabled. I made the rope carefully fast around his body, and charged him not to let go the ship till the sea came and took him off, and to mind and keep himself on top of the wave, which he did and passed on shore without much difficulty. In like manner all, fifteen in number, were conveyed safe on shore on what is called Cooldross Beach, eight miles from Weeklow Light, south-west of us, and sixteen miles from the city of Dublin, north-east of us, on the first day of

February, 1811, after a rough and boisterous passage of thirty days.

Here we remained about one month getting our lumber on shore, stripping our ship, and saving everything for the good of the underwriters as the case might be. I will here just say that after getting safe on shore and drying ourselves by the fire of a poor Irishman, who lived near by in a mud hut, and getting some refreshment in a better house near by, we returned to the ship, that is, those who were not too much exhausted with the labors of the day, and got the small anchor on shore with the cable attached, to prevent the ship from going off in case she should float the next tide.

The captain in the meantime procured a corporal and twelve men to guard the ship till morning. After getting all our charts, trunks, and private property on shore, and piling it up in the hut above named, we went to a certain house, and took lodgings in their barn for the night, where we obtained some few hours' sleep, the first we had enjoyed for some considerable length of time.

The first thing in the morning was for each one to look after their own things. In overhauling for mine I missed my trunks, which were stolen during the night by some of the Irish people who came down to the ship that night on purpose to plunder whatever might come to hand.

This trunk had in it all my best clothes. I also lost a pea jacket, for which I paid twenty dollars, boots, etc., in all worth about one hundred and fifty dollars. But seeing all our lives were spared I felt thankful to think we came off so well as we did. In this neighborhood we found a good boarding place, where the captain and myself boarded, except they had no floor, only one strip of board which ran alongside of the bed where we stood to dress and undress, all the rest being nothing more than smooth cement, which in damp weather becomes somewhat muddy, The crew and second mate took their meals on the beach, where the ship's cooking apparatus and provisions were landed.

After being here some days, I told a gentleman who came down to the ship about losing my trunk, and he said he would try to do something about it for me. Accordingly, he got all the priests in the vicinity a distance of eight miles from the ship each way to cry it in their churches.

These catholic priests told their congregations that if any of them had the American mate's trunk, or anything else belonging to the ship, to return it immediately, on pain of being excluded from the church. This declaration had some effect, but not the desired effect. The same gentleman, one morning, on going to his front door, saw a letter lying on the door-stone, which he took up, and read as follows: " Dear Sir: In the third crotch of such a tree in your garden you will find the American mate's pocket book." This pocket book, after being rifled of what money it contained, was all the thief would give up. And this is all I ever heard about it, or ever expect to.

This is a beautiful country, never very cold and never very hot. No sellers are needed here. Potatoes are dug and heaped up in the field, and covered over with a thin layer of earth, where they remain all winter or until they are wanted for use. Their manner of fattening lambs is somewhat curious; while but a few days old they are taken entirely away from the dam, and fed on cow's milk till about six weeks old, when they are considered fit for market. After milking the cow, the girl takes her seat, the pail of milk sitting by her side, with a tin dipper in it for the purpose, the boy takes the lamb from one pen, handing them to the girl, who with her dipper fills her mouth with the warm milk directly from the cow, and with the lamb on his back between her feet, her mouth to the lamb's mouth, she discharges mouthful after mouthful into the lamb's mouth, till he has received his allowance, when he is passed by another boy into the opposite pen. It is astonishing to see how quick this process of feeding lambs is accomplished.

A jury of carpenters from Dublin, after thoroughly examining our ship, reported that it would not be for the benefit of either owners or underwriters to attempt to get the ship off or to repair her at all. Most of her floor timbers being broken, besides being badly hogged and filled with water every high water, consequently a day being set, she was sold where she lay to the highest bidder, a gentleman from Dublin, for the meagre sum of two hundred and twenty pounds Irish currency or about nine hundred dollars.

Having done up all that there was for us to do in this place, we took the stage to Dublin, where I had been a few days before, and procured a voyage on board an American brig bound to Lisbon, the captain of which had some time before turned both of his mates on shore for some neglect on their part, which resulted in a lawsuit about some embezzlement of wine taken on board the brig, that the lumpers who stowed the cargo were found making too free with. Kind Providence again seemed to favor my brother and myself, for instead of losing any time by being cast away, we gained a day or two, not being paid off by the consignee from the ship we lost, till we had belonged to the brig a short time. And than we entered on board the brig in the same capacity that we had been in on board the ship, and having the same wages. And, having no bills of lading to sign, the brig being already loaded and ready for sea, we had rather an easy time of it. This brig belonged to Abial Wood, of Wiscasset, Edward Langdon, Master, and had taken in a cargo of barley, hams, wine, etc., for Lord Wellington's army, which was then only about fifty miles from Lisbon contending with the world-renowned Bonaparte. The barley was intended for his horses.

We had a good passage to Lisbon, only we had a comical man for our captain, whom we found it necessary to check a little in regard to his conduct with the steward and the boy, towards whom he seemed to be rather unkind.

We discharged this cargo into lighters that came

along side to receive it in a few days, and then went down south about seventy-five miles to St. Tubes for a cargo of salt. Here, during the captain's absence to Lisbon, attending his lawsuit, we hauled the brig on shore and smoked her, in order to destroy the rats that had become very annoying; indeed, so much so that it was difficult sleeping on account of them in the night. This smoking business was accomplished in the following manner: The windows and companion way were closed, the hatches put on, after making three fires in the hold, one forward, one aft, and one amidships; blue clay was had in readiness, and then a man with three parcels of sulphur in his hands, and a rope secured round his body, so that if he should be suffocated before reaching the deck we could draw him out, went into the hold and threw the sulphur into the several fires and returned on deck, when the hatches were clapped on and this blue clay put into the seams to make them perfectly tight so that no smoke could escape. This was done precisely at ten A. M., when all was tight as a cup. At twelve M., just two hours from the time the hatches were put on, they were again taken off, and the smoke permitted to escape. When all was gone so that it was safe to go below, we ventured cautiously down into the hold, when lo and behold! there they lay, rank and file, side by side, like so many slain soldiers, round the several fires, no less than two hundred and seventy rats of all sizes, from about the size of a mouse up to the bigness of a decent sized cat; and not only were the rats and mice all destroyed, but every thing, bugs, spiders, flies — whatever had or was liable to have animal life was completely destroyed, so that we had no more trouble from this direction. It may be proper for me here to say that the paint in the cabin and wherever else there was any, was also entirely ruined.

Here we were on the Fourth of July, the day of our national independence. American ships in this port had their colors flying, their cannon roaring, and sailors on shore had abundance of drinking, fighting, and such like other carnal mirth and merriment as suited them best.

After taking in our cargo of salt, we bent sails and prepared for sea; and about the last day of July, 1811, we weighed anchor and sailed for Boston, and after a fair weather passage of some thirty-five or forty days we arrived safe once more in the United States, from which I had been absent about nine months.

After receiving my pay for my services on board the brig, I took passage in a coasting vessel to Castine, and found my family all well, though almost out of patience waiting my return. This was my last voyage.

CHAPTER V.

Those familiar with the scenes of those days will recollect that in 1812 war with Great Britain was declared by President Madison. This, of course, put an end to all commercial intercourse with other nations, except in cases where merchants and ship owners were disposed, for the sake of gain, to run the risk of being taken by English cruisers or of fighting their way through on their own hook. This I am glad to say many did, some by beating off their assailants and others by retaking their vessels after they had been taken possession of by the enemy.

After being peaceably settled at home with my little family, I concluded, having some money to spare for that purpose, to finish another room in my house. Accordingly I engaged a carpenter and set him about the work, and, when ready, had it plastered, etc. And now commences a new era in my life.

I will here say to the reader that I now, on this page, in the beginning of this chapter, commence writing what I call my Christian experience.

I am aware of the responsibility and difficulty of this undertaking, inasmuch as I am not learned, and but little used to writing for the press. It will be with difficulty that I shall make this subject as plain and intelligent to the interested reader as I have a desire to. But one thing I promise, and that is, I will do the best I can, hoping and praying that the grace of the Lord Jesus Christ will be with the writer and the reader, so that both shall be profited in writing and in reading what follows in the relation of this humble effort of the writer to contribute something subservient to the cause of truth.

In speaking of some of the incidents of my childhood, the reader will probably recollect that I spoke of hearing a sermon preached by the Rev. Daniel Merrill, when I was about twelve years of age, on the terrible condition of the lost sinner in a future state. I also spoke of the astonishing effect it had on my mind, causing me to weep profusely, etc. Although these solemn truths, as I then considered, and still believe them to be, were not lasting in their influence on my mind, being, as it were, supplanted by youthful follies and indulgencies, yet I think they were of some benefit to me, for I never saw the time in my life that I felt pleased at hearing religion spoken against.

The next time that I now recollect of feeling serious about my soul, was when about twenty years of age, after my arrival home from that three years and a half cruise, that I spoke of having been cast away in an English man-of-war. I heard a sermon about this time preached by the Rev. John Burnham, of Orland, a Baptist minister. His text was 1 Peter 4 : 18. "And if the righteous scarcely be saved, where shall the ungodly and the sinner appear?" I distinctly recollect to this day how he handled this subject; and I would that ministers at the present day would be as plain, as pointed, and as exact in their preaching as was this servant of Christ (I mean some of them). After introducing his subject, he said, "I shall now proceed to contrast characters," which he did with such force and clearness as made his hearers conclude that the subject was one not to be trifled with. I remember now to this day, although it is fifty-five years since, a remark that I made to my shipmates, as we together were passing out of the house. I said, "If the speaker has told us the truth to night, we are in an evil case," to which one of them replied, "I guess you are going to be a Methodist." This was a solemn meeting, and I have no doubt it did good. But the impressions made on my mind were like the morning cloud or the early dew;—they soon passed away.

The next rather singular event that I now think of in reference to my serious impressions was on this wise: A meeting having been held at my father's one Sabbath, on retiring to bed with a Deacon Weed, a very pious man, who had taken an active part in the evening meeting, he said, as we were about getting into bed, "Lord, I am going to bed with this impenitent sinner, and perhaps he is a better man by nature than I am" Nothing farther was said, and we were both soon asleep. In the morning, as the day broke, I awoke out of sleep with a most singular groan, which surprised me not a little, and for which I could never account. In a few minutes the old gentleman arose and dressed himself and went into the room where my mother was getting breakfast, and said to her, so loud that I distinctly heard every word, "That son of yours is going to be a Christian." My mother replied, "What makes you think so, Deacon Weed?" "Because," said he, "I asked the Lord if he would make him a Christian to make him groan; and he immediately groaned out three times." This I heard and have, as simple as it might appear to others, often thought of it myself.

Sometimes in distressing gales at sea, I used to pray as I lay in my berth, when it was my watch below. Once when at home at my father's in time of a religious awakening in the place, I became so far sensible of my lost condition as a sinner, and the need I stood in of something that I had not, that I went out one morning alone and knelt down, and tried to pray as well as I could, but it seemed hard work; I rose up and left the place with a measure of disappointment and even disgust, very much cast down and discouraged in my mind, and almost ready to think God a hard master and an austere sovereign. On my way back to the house a verse of Dr. Watts' poetry struck my mind with great weight and solemnity, so much so that I seemed to settle under it, and came near crying out to God to have mercy on my soul, which if I had, I now think, it would have been much more acceptable to God than any form of prayer that I could make up of myself; but I was not aware of that at the time.

The words of the hymn I will here express:

> The fearful soul that tires and faints,
>   And walks the ways of God no more,
> Is but esteemed almost a saint,
>   And makes his own destruction sure.

As I have just said, these words came near bringing me to the ground. They were to me like a clap of thunder in a clear sky, awfully alarming and significant; but what could I do? I had just been trying to pray as well as I could; I could not tell *what* to do, but, dear reader, I will tell you what I did do — I did as thousands before me had done, and as thousands since have done. I said to the blessed spirit, as one said a good many hundred years ago to an inspired apostle, "Go thy way for this time; when I have a more convenient season I will call for thee." Acts 24:25, last clause.

The reader may say, "What *could* you have done?" I will tell you what I might have done. I might right there on the spot, before returning to the house, have smote on my breast and cried, "God be merciful to me a sinner," and this was just what God wanted done, for it was a time of reformation in the place, and many were enquiring what they should do to be saved, and they needed this example of penitence set before them to stimulate and encourage them to seek the Lord then, while he was to be found, and to call on him while he was near. Besides, had I thus obeyed the Spirit instead of quenching its holy influence, I might returned to the house rejoicing in a Saviour's love. But instead of this I put the Saviour off for the present, by promising, if he would let me go one voyage more and return safe, I would then attend to the great salvation, become a Christian, have prayers in my family, and be a religious man.

Having made this promise conscience became quiet, and I thought but little about it till I returned home again from Liverpool in the ship in which I was finally cast away. Then conscience would say, "now fulfil your promise, become religious, and pray in your family." But no; I was not quite ready yet. One voyage more, and then. Thus I went on procrastinating. But the second voyage was a terrible one. It was the one in which I buried my dear brother in the midst of the ocean. I have already told you what a terrible day that was to me — the day on which he died. But I made no new promises — I knew that would be insulting God. So I made the best of it I could, and finally returned safe again, reckless of former vows. I went on as usual till I entered upon the last voyage — the one on which I was cast away and barely escaped with my life. After returning from this long and perilous voyage in which I came so very near losing my life, instead of feeling thankful to my kind preserver, I was farther from it than ever. So much so that my affectionate wife took notice of it, and spoke about it one day to me, saying: "It appears to me, husband, that you are more thoughtless and indifferent about religious things than I ever knew you to be." I replied, it was even so, and why it should be so I could not tell; but certain it was I had reached a climax in my career of folly in which I felt no fear of God or man, though I felt no disposition to do wrong or to injure any one, treated everybody respectfully, and seemed to think that all was well, and that I should never be in adversity. All my former conviction was gone, and all my solemn promises to Jehovah about entirely forgotten. Things went on smoothly in this way for some weeks, and I was quite contented with the condition of affairs around me.

One evening while keeping a moderate fire in the parlor to dry the plastering, I was singing to several of my younger brothers one of my old favorite sea songs, when suddenly a shock struck my mind to stop. At that moment (for it was all the work of a moment) I saw in my imagination a very small substance, not larger than a lady's thimble, start, as it were, from the sky, the eye of my mind being upon it while it came to me and seemed to lodge within me, not, however, affecting me in the least. I took no more notice of it then, neither have I since up to the present day, only to remember that it was in my imagination just so. Whether it was absolutely anything or nothing, I cannot say. I merely mention it as something that passed through my mind at the moment. I relate it as no part of my Christian experience, but I do say, from that moment what I call my Christian experience commenced.

A brother younger than I said to me, "Why don't you finish singing that song, brother Lemuel?" for there had been perfect silence for about one minute. I replied to him that I should never sing another carnal song while earth was my abode. That was forty-nine years ago, and I have never broken that promise, if indeed it was a promise. Nothing further took place that evening. Early the next morning, before the sun arose, the birds in the grove might have seen me on bended knees, engaged in solemn prayer to Almighty God, that he would spare me long enough to repent of my sins and secure the salvation of my soul. From that blessed day up to the present morning I have been a man of prayer.

I did not obtain repentance or forgiveness immediately, though, like Esau, I sought it carefully with tears. But one thing I resolved to do, and that was, to seek for it the remainder of my days, whether they should be few or many. I had a great deal to look over — I had been a great offender — there was a terrible black catalogue against me. There was disobedience to my parents — no small item in this dark record of wickedness I had to overhaul; a lack of kindness to brothers and sisters, playmates, schoolfellows, and such like; now and then a falsehood, and sometimes a deliberate lie even, were to be seen floating on the wake of my past live; profane swearing, also, was here and there to be seen on the past; late hours when I ought to have been on shipboard; the card table, the dancing floor, and a measure of intemperate eating and drinking; besides, the many sins of omission, such as neglect of the Bible and religious worship, and doing good to others when I had an opportunity. All these, and many more that might be named, were in the past, and must be repented of or remain as dead weights to sink the soul down deeper and deeper, where hope nor mercy could never come.

But the greatest difficulty of all in the way of my salvation I found to be within, and I could say as another has said before me:

> "Here on my heart the burden lies,
> While past offences pain my eyes."

Indeed, the language of my heart was "What must I do to be saved?" I read the Scriptures carefully, and the more I read them the more sure I was of their Divine origin, for I knew that no man or set of men could have portrayed my character and condition with such exactness as they did; and the more I read the worse I appeared to myself, for they did indeed show myself to myself. I found myself condemned already, and the wrath of God abiding upon me.

There was no revival of religion in the place where I lived at this time, and no minister lived within miles of me. Once in a while, to be sure, a travelling minister would pass through our neighborhood and preach a lecture, but nothing seemed to reach my case. Christians there were in the place, who sometimes spoke an encouraging word to me, and told me they thought I should have religion before long. Sometimes my heart would seem to be so hard that nothing could affect it. And then there was so much unbelief, and so much pride, I seemed to be bound, as it were, hand and foot, and had no power to extricate myself from this awful dilemma into which I found myself plunged by my sin. But I continued to hope that I should find relief sooner or later. Prayer was sometimes almost a burden, and there was such a want of sincerity in it that I could have no confidence in it, or anything else that I could do.

The fear of hell and a future state was not what troubled me, though there might have been something of that kind mixed in with my trouble. But the principal difficulty with me was unreconciliation to God. We seemed to be antagonistical to each other, and my poor heart in spite of myself seemed to rebel against the Lord, and this it was that distressed me.

And after trying many days and nights to make myself better, and finding that I, if anything, grew worse, I came to the conclusion that all efforts in this direction were vain, I perceived that justification by the law could not be, that my righteousness was but worthless rags compared with the requirements of the divine law, which was holy, just and good, while I was carnal, sold under sin; "For the good that I would I did not, and what I hated that I did." Rom. 7 : 15.

About this time, having lost all confidence in my own works, though I continued to try to pray as well as I could, I felt so distressed that I cried right out in the presence of my wife one evening, and said: O that God would come this night and have mercy on my poor soul. This was something different from whatever I had done before; it gave my wife a sudden shock, being so unlooked for from such a person as I was. To say the least, I think it was not more than twenty or thirty minutes after this solemn ejaculation in the hearing of my companion before my mind was suddenly caught away, and I was carried as quick as thought to take a retrospective view of the past events of my life, while on the high seas — the many dangers I had passed through, the wonderful deliverances I had experienced at the hand of God, when in the utmost danger aloft reefing top gallant sails while braces were parting, sails slatting, the yards flying, while facing the cannon's mouth, shot whistling by me, men dying around me, dying with fevers, repeatedly cast upon a lee shore, drawn safe to land by a single rope, on a foreign shore, and all that sort of thing. I say almost as quick as thought these scenes passed before me in rapid succession, giving me such a striking discovery of the matchless power and goodness of God in my preservations as I never had before. I at this moment for the first time discovered that God was good, supremely good, and *that* goodness affected my heart as it never had been before. It broke it all down, so that I exclaimed aloud in astonishment, "O, how good the Lord is!" I understood now better than ever before what the Scripture means when it says, Rom. 2 : 4, "Not knowing that the goodness of God leadeth thee to repentance." But it did lead me to repentance unto life, never to be repented of. From that good hour I have known better than ever to indulge any hard thoughts of God. All my self-will and impudent stubbornness was gone; I felt completely reconciled to God, and willing to be in his hand like clay in the hands of the potter. The way of life and salvation through the Lord Jesus Christ appeared so glorious that I felt perfectly safe and happy. My mind, which before for days and weeks had been like the troubled sea when it cannot rest, at once became quiet and peaceful, and all through soul, body and spirit I experienced a great calm.

I found that being justified by faith, I had peace with God, through our Lord Jesus Christ. And having had but little rest for a number of nights previous to this, I soon fell into a quiet sleep, from which I did not awake till the morning light shone into my window.

On awaking I immediately arose, made a fire, and took and opened my Bible. The exact place opened to I do not now recollect, but I was astonished to perceive how different it read from what it ever did before. Instead of being against me it now was for me, instead of condemning it now justified me; in a word, it seemed like a new book. But I soon closed it, and hasted away to my father's some half a mile distance, to let him know what great things God had done for me. When passing by my brother's house he wanted to know why I made such haste. I told him I was going to tell my father what I had experienced. He said, "Why not tell me?" I told him he would not understand me if I should, and hurried on to tell him who had offered up so many prayers in my behalf, how the good Lord had heard and answered them all in bringing me to the knowledge of the truth as it is in Jesus.

When I entered the house my father was just making the fire on the hearth. As I spoke he looked up at me, and when I had finished what I then had to say, he replied, with tears, "I think, Lemuel, you have good reason for a hope." I hardly comprehended what he meant by a hope, though his remark was exactly what it should be, but I was rejoicing in the God of my salvation, therefore I could hardly understand what the word hope meant. Others soon came into the kitchen, and we rejoiced together in God. I want the reader of my Christian experience as I have here now related it to understand that on the twelfth day of January, 1812, at about nine o'clock in the evening, I was born again, and translated from the kingdom of darkness into the kingdom of God's dear Son; that I then passed from death unto life, — that old things passed away and that to me all things became new, — and that all things were of God, who made all things, and who, of his own will, had made me a new creature in Christ Jesus, and that it was wholly to the praise of the glory of his grace that I had become a Christian; for had he never called after me again after I was shipwrecked and returned home the last time, I should never have become a true believer in the Lord Jesus Christ, but should have died in my sins, and where Christ is gone I should never have come.

What reason I have to praise the Lord who by the power of His grace (not by works of righteousness which I had done) snatched me as a brand from the burning, and put a new song into my mouth, even praise unto God.

The June following, which was in 1812, receiving an invitation to unite with the Baptist Church in a neighboring town, I told the minister I must read the New Testament carefully through to know which of the two churches was right about baptism, for I felt it my duty to be baptized, and as there was a Baptist Church and a Congregational Church both a like distance from me, and as they differed very much about this holy ordinance of the church of God, I wanted exceedingly to know which of the two was right; accordingly I wanted time to read for myself.

My anxiety for sinners that they might come to Christ and have salvation was very great, and it somehow appeared to me as though I could tell them just how to proceed in order to be converted, and this I often tried to do. But it all seemed strange to them; they could not understand the things of the spirit, because they are spiritually discerned.

I was holding prayer meetings in the neighborhood where I lived as often as once a week. In these I used to read a sermon from a book entitled Burder's Village Sermons, and excellent sermons they were too. I used to enter so fully into the spirit of them while reading that the people seemed to take about the same interest in them as though the author of them had been present delivering them himself. After getting through with the sermon, I used frequently to make some further remarks in connection with the subject treated in the sermon, which I think were also well received.

Soon after my conversion it was impressed upon my mind to pray in my family. This seemed to be very crossing, and I hardly knew how to begin this work of family religion, yet I felt satisfied it was my duty to read my Bible and pray with my family. Finally, I set a day to commence. On the Lord's day morning I thought would be a suitable time for that purpose, but when the morning came my reluctance was so great that I put it off for another week, and when the second Sabbath came aversion to this duty still continued. I promised once more that the next Sabbath day should find me on my knees engaged in prayer with and for my family; but when the day came, notwithstanding I had been praying to God every day in secret to give me strength to take up this cross, I strangely dreaded to try to pray before my wife and two or three little children that we then had.

When I awoke from sleep it came with force on my mind that I must pray in my family that day or displease God. This I could not think of doing, so I resolved, live or die, I would try to pray in the evening. Towards night, having at hand a book in which there was some family prayers, I thought I would write off one of these, making such alterations as would render the prayer appropriate to our circumstances, and would commit it to memory, and would kneel down and say that. Accordingly, I commenced writing and wrote ten lines across the paper, and thought I would commit that to memory first and then write and commit the remainder, but to my utter astonishment I could not commit a single line. I folded it up and put it into the fire, rose up, knelt down on the floor, and there for the first time in the presence of any one I prayed as well as I could with such words as I could command, and then rose up feeling some better in my mind for having obeyed the Lord to the best of my ability in that thing. But oh! alas! what a prayer was that. It seemed to have neither beginning nor end, nor anything else. I was astonished to think I could not pray better than that, and felt pity for my poor wife that she should have to hear such language addressed to the Almighty.

Anxiety for sinners increased so in my mind that I thought to try to have prayer meetings in the neighborhood; and, with the advice of others, I commenced holding evening meetings. In these I used to read to the people Burder's Village Sermons, which were very suitable on such occasions, and were listened to with great interest by the people.

Young people and all classes flocked to these meetings, and they seemed to be attended with much interest. An aged Baptist deacon called one day to see me, and while relating to him some of my experience, and how I believed the atonement intended alike for all, he remarked that if he believed so, he should be a Universalist. This gave me a terrible shock, for I could not believe in Universalism any how, it was so contrary to what the Bible had taught me. But as the Bible taught me that Christ tasted death for every man, that He gave His life a ransom for all, and that whosoever believed on Him should not perish, but should have everlasting life, I came to the conclusion that the only reason why one was saved and another lost was just simply because one believed and obeyed the Gospel, while another did not.

With these views of Divine truth, I went on trying to persuade sinners to believe in the Saviour, and whenever I had an opportunity to speak in any meeting after hearing a sermon, I used to try to impress it on the mind of sinners that they were to blame for not repenting and believing in the Lord Jesus Christ.

In June, after my conversion in January, Father Case came into the neighborhood and held some meetings. I listened to his preaching with great interest. He was an aged minister of the Gospel of Christ, and although not very learned he was very pious, and his labors were greatly blessed wherever he preached. He gave me some good advice, and on leaving in the morning after putting up with me all night, he said he hoped I should take up my cross and follow Christ and be baptized. This I was willing to do as soon as I could find out which of the two denominations were right about what constituted baptism, as there were

Baptist and Congregational Churches in the neighboring town of Sedgwick, where I should have to go in order to unite with some church, which I thought it was my duty to do. Accordingly I commenced reading the New Testament for that purpose, to find out whether in the days of the apostles, they baptized people by sprinkling or by immersion, and having read very carefully to the sixth chapter of Romans, and while reading in that what the apostle says in the fourth and fifth verses, I found no occasion to read any farther for that purpose, but with perfect ease perceived that nothing short of entire immersion of the whole body in water could answer the design of water baptism. Accordingly soon after this I was received into the Baptist Church of Christ, in Sedgwick, and baptized by the venerable father Case.

I remained a member of this church, until a number of us was dismissed from it, to help constitute a church in Brooksville, where the Lord had poured out the Holy Spirit, and converted a goodly number of souls in the vicinity where I resided, and where I had been converted some five years before.

In those days there was one thing that used to astonish me as much, and perhaps I might say more, than any one thing else, and that was, good people appeared to take so little interest in the welfare of sinners. I used, when seeing a good brother or a deacon passing step to the road, and speak to him about the goodness of God, and how happy I felt in his love, but to my surprise instead of joining me in this, he or they would often reply by saying: "Well, brother Norton, you are living on your bounty money now; you won't always feel as you do now," and so the subject would be laid aside, and something else introduced instead of it, or the brother would pass on his way.

Though this would sometimes cool my zeal for the time being, yet it never had any lasting effect on my mind. I knew the religion of Christ would never wear out, that it was more precious than gold, yea than much fine gold. And that whatever it might be to others, it was every thing to me.

I wanted every person young and old to share in its blessedness, for well I knew, that no one could be happy without it, and that having it, all other things would be added to it; this I was plainly taught in the Scriptures of divine truth.

I sometimes felt astonished that even ministers of the Gospel appeared to take no more interest in the conversion of precious souls. I recollect one that I thought much of, (and indeed I thought much of them all, and have to this day, with a very few exceptions) to appoint a meeting at my house, and come and preach to us, and I would circulate the notice, and have as many attend as possible. Accordingly he did. When the evening arrived the house was well filled. The preacher, as I thought, preached well making use of some of the very arguments to persuade sinners to seek the Lord, that I had in my own mind, that I supposed no one but myself had ever thought of. There I sat, expecting every minute when I should see tears flow, and hear some poor soul cry out for mercy, when in fact they sat there as unmoved as if some boy had been playing on a jewsharp.

I then began to sink in my expectations, and tried as well as I could to account for this dreadful apathy among sinners, and I came to the conclusion that they had eyes but did not see, that they had ears but they did not hear. This led me to think of this text: "Hear and your soul shall live" (Isaiah 4:3). But there was one fact that astonished me more than everything else connected with this meeting. The truth that had been preached that evening by that servant of Christ I knew to be the Gospel, and that it would be a savor of life unto life or of death unto death unto those who heard it, and seeing so little prospect of its doing good, it caused me to feel sad even to weeping; but that minister appeared perfectly satisfied with the meeting, and with everybody who attended it. This was more than I could then understand, and in fact, I never to this day, have been able to understand how ministers, who profess to believe that the Gospel is God's last remedy for man's salvation, and that it is certain to kill or cure, that is to say, to make people better or worse — I say, how any one can administer this powerful prescription, so to speak, and yet feel a measure of indifference about the effect produced, is something that is to me quite inexplicable.

In the summer of 1816 there was a glorious revival of religion in the town of Sedgwick, about six or seven miles east of my place of residence. Having a great desire to see some young converts, as I had never seen one since my conversion, I immediately, on hearing that a number of young persons had experienced religion, went over to see them, and so strong was my affection for these young disciples of the Lord Jesus, that I was loth to leave the place. I rejoiced with them with great joy. Here I want to say, that notwithstanding what great things God had done for me in taking me out of the horrible pit and miry clay of sin, and bringing me into the glorious light and liberty of the Gospel — I say, notwithstanding all this, I frequently had doubts and fears lest after all I might be deceived, and have taken up with something short of saving conversion to God, but among these young converts I had all my doubts and fears removed. I loved them so well that I knew I had passed from death unto life, because I loved the brethren. After remaining a few days with them, I went home rejoicing, on account of what the Lord was doing in that place, but oh! how strong was my desire that He would in mercy visit Brooksville!

Soon after returning home I was called upon to stay one night with an aged person who was very sick. The night following she died, I suppose without any hope in Christ. At her funeral, after the sermon, I arose and made a few remarks about the importance of seeking religion while in youth. Tears flowed freely from many eyes, and the result of that person's death was the striking under conviction of seven young men, who afterwards were brought to rejoice in the God of their salvation. From this the work of the Lord commenced, and a glorious revival of religion followed, in which many scores of sinners were brought from darkness to light, and from the power and dominion of sin into the glorious light and liberty of the Gospel.

My mind at this time was greatly exercised about entering more fully into the work of trying to save — that is, trying instrumentally — to save souls; so much so that I wanted to be all the while employed about something either directly or indirectly connected with this great and glorious work. Every now and then texts of Scripture would strike my mind with great force. I would see such beauty and glory in the plan of salvation as would lead me to have a strong desire to go and tell others of those precious truths. I thought to be a minister of the Gospel was one of the greatest blessings, the greatest privileges, a mortal man could come into possession of in this world, and that I would prefer being a humble minister of the Gospel than to be a king on a throne. Indeed, I had such a desire for the work of a Minister of Christ that at times it became almost overwhelming, while at the same time it looked almost impossible that one so far removed from any qualifications whatever for such a a holy work could ever be successful if they engaged in it. I often thought of one expression of the Apostle Paul: "If any man desire the office of a bishop, he desireth a good work" (1 Timothy 3:1).

The apostle then goes on to say what the qualifications of a bishop must be.

I have no doubt now but that the Lord was then calling me to the work of the ministry, though I was not fully aware of it at that time. My brethren in the church had such thoughts at that time, as they have since told me. I never heard any voice speaking to me as one man speaks to another, saying, " Go thou and preach the kingdom of God," but I had the Holy Spirit operating powerfully within me, showing me the lost state of sinners, and how much they needed the Gospel in order that they might be saved. The church and people of God, I perceived, needed the sincere milk of the Word, that they might grow thereby.

I used to improve my gift as well as I could when an opportunity presented, in trying to encourage young converts especially to persevere, and older saints to be up and doing, working out their own salvation with fear and trembling. And some times I did take great satisfaction in so doing; at other times it would be very different with me, and I would be afraid that I had done more hurt than good by speaking. Still there seemed to be a propelling power urging me forward to speak, so that if I, through the fear of man or from any other consideration, neglected my duty in this way, I would leave the meeting under great dejection of mind, feeling more like a criminal than anything else.

There seemed to be a strange inconsistency in my

mind. I seemed to be in a strait between two opposing inclinations, one to go forward and try to teach sinners the way of salvation — the other to be silent and say nothing to them.

I carefully watched the providences of God, and whatever they indicated I considered of importance in coming to a decision on this important question of duty, for it had now become a subject of solemn enquiry whether it was my duty to commence trying to preach the Gospel or not. Many things seemed to favor such a course — other things looked unfavorable. When I did try to speak in meeting, it was heard with interest by the people, and seemed to edify and benefit them, though it would look very poor to me.

One forbidding circumstance was, I had a family to provide for, and I never had the most distant thought of any pecuniary aid for preaching until after I engaged in the work.

But the great question with me was, "Does the good Lord require it of you to go and as much as in you is, to preach the kingdom of God?" Here was the question. "No man, no matter what his talents or his abilities in other respects are, has any right to take this honor to himself any more than Aaron had." (Thess. 5:4).

In order that I might enjoy every possible facility for deciding this great question, my brethren, when there was an ordination called for anywhere in the vicinity and a delegation from the church requested, would be sure and send me as one of that number, that I might hear the experience of others who were about being inducted into the sacred office. Whether these opportunities were of much benefit to me or not, I can hardly say. I recollect one time, however, of going to attend the ordination of the Rev. Edward Carter, of West Brooksville, where a very interesting season of public worship was enjoyed. After the ordination was attended to, while making my way home through a piece of lonely woods, my mind being absorbed on the question of duty — whether I was willing to go and preach the kingdom of God or no, provided the Lord required it of me. All at once there appeared in my imagination a flock of lambs, every other one of which was so poor in flesh, and withal so feeble for the want of suitable food, that they greatly excited my pity, and I began to conclude if they were all in this miserable condition, I would try some how or other to relieve them. While casting about in my mind how this could be done, they at once became converts, and every one of them as poor as the poorest. This affected me exceedingly. Duty now stared me in the face. These converts represented everybody who was starving for the want of that Gospel which I had received of the Lord Jesus, and which I ought to preach. I then and there concluded that I would henceforth try to preach the Gospel.

In 1817, on Thanksgiving Day, was the first time that I took a text and tried to explain it to the church.

The day previous to this I was returning home from a journey, and while travelling along the road alone, these words passed gently through my mind: "Only fear the Lord, and serve him in truth, with all your heart; for consider how great things he hath done for you" (1 Samuel 12:24). These words, so full of precious truth, so full of encouragement to the church and people of God, looked to me very suitable for the foundation of a religious discourse for the next day, being Thanksgiving Day. Accordingly I resolved on making some remarks from these words if an opportunity was given. Having no pastor, we held social meetings, where every one had the privilege of improving their gift as they thought proper. Being clerk of the church, the deacons put it to me to read for the church. On being assembled together at the usual hour, the acting deacon passed the Bible to my hand, requesting me to read a certain Psalm which he named, observing at the same time that if I had any light upon it, or any other passage of Scripture, he would like to have me make some remarks therefrom. This was precisely what I wanted to hear him say, though I had often heard him say the same before. Accordingly, after reading the Psalm alluded to, I turned to the text above named, and read with much solemnity those precious words which had been food to my hungry soul the day before. And if ever words found place in every heart, these I think did, for the attention given to them and to what followed was profound indeed.

I remarked, *First*, What God had done for his ancient people, and what he had done for us.

Secondly, What a little he required of us in return.

Thirdly, What that little was, merely to fear him and to be sincere and thorough in our service to him.

I spoke just twenty minutes from these words with much freedom, when all at once I found nothing further to say, and took my seat. From this day forward it was understood that I had commenced preaching the Gospel, a fact that I had no desire to contradict.

On the sixteenth of January, 1817, the church thought proper to give me license to preach the Gospel, and that the reader may here see how such a thing was done forty-four years ago, I will transcribe into this book the entire license, which now lies before me:

To all whom it may concern:
This is to certify that the bearer, Lemuel Norton, is a member of this church in regular standing, and having a belief that the Lord has called him to preach the Gospel, and we having gained satisfactory evidence of the same, do this day grant him license to go forth in the strength of the Lord and improve his gift in that way which he shall think to be most for the glory of God, the advancement of the Redeemer's kingdom, and the good of immortal souls. Our prayers go with him that the Lord will ever be with, strengthen, encourage, and enable him to perform the arduous work of the ministry with faithfulness and zeal; that he may see the pleasure of the Lord prosper in his hands. And now, brethren and people, we recommend him to you. Receive him as the servant of Christ, and as the laborer is worthy of his hire, and those that preach the gospel

should live by the Gospel, you will grant him all that encouragement and assistance which the nature of his situation and circumstances may require.

Done in behalf of the Second Baptist Church in Sedgwick, January 16th, 1817.

   Signed by order of the Church,
     AMOS ALLEN, Pastor.
     SOLOMON BILLINGS, } Deacons.
     ABEL BILLINGS,

After this I used to hold meetings in different places, wherever it appeared to be my duty, and where the people desired it — frequently in my father's house, and wherever there was a destitute church I used to supply them occasionally. On one occasion I preached at my father's house on the Sabbath from the text, "Unto you, therefore, which believe, He is precious" (1 Peter 2:7). I enjoyed much freedom in speaking from these words. One woman, who seemed rather puzzled at hearing others speak favorably of the discourse, said she had the sermon at home in her house.

About a year after I experienced religion, my brother Noah, who afterwards became a Baptist minister, experienced the same grace, and my wife also; they were baptized soon after by Rev. Lemuel Jackson, a travelling minister, and an excellent good man.

One special providence of God, which I ought to have related before, I will introduce now. Immediately after peace with Great Britain, after the war of 1812 took place, I was called upon to help rig and fit for sea the largest ship ever built at Castine, and had agreed to go out first mate of her. This was before I commenced to preach the gospel. While preparing this ship for sea I boarded with the man who built her about three weeks. She was a well built ship, new and strong, but from some cause or other, I could not tell why, I felt as though it would not be best for me to go to sea in that ship, and not only so, but that it would not be *safe* for me to go in her. So strong was this impression on my mind that I could not rest well in my sleep at night. Finally, a day or two before the ship was ready for sea, I told the owner I wanted him to let me off from going out in the ship; my things were already on board the ship, and I had been expecting all the time to go in her. The owner was some surprised to discover my disinclination to go, and wanted an explanation. I told him I had none to give, but that if he would give me up, and consider our agreement null and void, I would find a man to take my place, who I had no doubt would be entirely acceptable to the captain and to all concerned. To this he finally agreed. A brother of mine, younger than I, who was about to go, when he perceived that I was not going in the ship, wished to know if I thought he had better go or not. I told him I could not advise him at all about it, but to do as he thought best under the circumstances. He went — they all went — but never returned. The ship was sold in New York, the officers and crew took passage in a schooner belonging in Portsmouth, bound to Boston. She went on shore off Boston Light and every soul, being twenty-two in all, perished, in a severe snow storm. When the sad tidings reached me one evening at the door of my house, no one can tell how I felt for my dear brother, who but a few weeks before, had so inquiringly asked my advice about going in that ship. And when I came to review my own feelings and impressions about going in her, I could but acknowledge the special interposition of Divine Providence in my escape; for had I have gone, I should have done as they did, and should have been lost. Never after this did I attempt a voyage at sea, but came to the conclusion that heaven had something else for me to do.

CHAPTER VI.

From the time I was licensed to preach, to the time of my ordination, I visited several islands of the sea in Penobscot Bay, among these were Vinalhaven and Islesborough. I hired a boat of one of my neighbors, and started one day for Vinalhaven; on my way thither, I met a head wind, and must either return home or go to Islesborough. I concluded to visit Islesborough, and soon found myself safely landed on that beautiful isle of the sea.

There I remained nine days, and preached eleven times. Their minister, the Rev. Lemuel Rich, had left them a few months before, and moved off. This rendered my visit very acceptable to them. This island is about twelve miles long, and all the way from one to two miles broad (containing seventy-five families). The people came from all parts of the Island to hear the converted sailor preach, who about seven years before, when mate of a ship, they had seen come on shore and with the captain take a seat in one of their pews, and listen to a sermon delivered by this same Mr. Rich we spoke of as having recently removed from the island. It was almost amusing to see with what intense interest they watched every gesture, and listened to every word that fell from the speaker's lips. Never shall I forget my feelings when ascending into that pulpit. I tried to think of the text, but not a word of that sermon could I possibly call to mind that I had heard only a few short years before delivered from that desk.

I could but think how different the position I now sustained, to what it was then. Then I entered that house as a wicked sailor, though mate of a fine ship that lay off the shore right in sight, within half a mile of the meeting house; now I entered it as a servant of the most high God, to show sinners the way of salvation, and spake to them from the blessed words: "It is good for me to draw nigh to God" (Pslams 73 : 28). Oh! how happy my soul felt while telling them of the blessedness of nearness to God. I was called upon while here to attend a funeral; a woman died and was brought to the middle of the island to be interred. The house was crowded. My text was: "Prepare to meet thy God." It was a weeping time. I noticed the lady of the house (for the meeting was in the house of the brother of the deceased) sat bathed in tears, all the while I was trying to set before them what constituted a preparation to meet God. After meeting, she informed me that she had till quite recently been living on an outer point of the island, where she did not enjoy the means of grace as some did, and that she prayed that the Lord would let her have a place to live somewhere on the main road, where she could have the privilege of taking care of some of Christ's ministers, and enjoy their society more frequently than she could where she then lived.

And that the Lord had answered that prayer — that her husband had recently purchased that farm and she had had her request granted — and that while I was speaking of what constituted a preparation to meet God, it was so exactly in accordance with her experience that she could not refrain from weeping, for she had been doubting her religious experience from time to time, but felt greatly encouraged from the remarks made from the text to hope that she was a Christian in deed and in truth, which I have no reason to doubt, her neighbors bearing witness that she was one of the excellent of the earth. I preached to this people occasionally for five years, and had the happiness of seeing many sinners converted to God and added to the church. I trust through my humble efforts in the cause of Immanuel.

Returning home from Islesborough, I next visited Mount Desert, where there had been some religious interest among the people, and a goodly number had found the Savior precious to their souls, and a small Baptist Church had been organized by Rev. Father Case and Rev. Bryant Linnen. In this place I stopped a number of Sabbaths, and preached with much freedom. Here was a large Congregational Church. Father Eaton was their minister, and had been for many years, though, being rather illiterate, he had never been ordained, because it was against their rules to ordain an illiterate man to the work of the ministry. Quite a number of this church had left and become Baptists, and joined the newly organized Baptist Church.

Returning home again, I soon after visited Vinalhaven, or Fox Island, as it was formerly called. The Baptist Church here, too, was destitute of a pastor, and I consented to labor with them a few Sabbaths.

After this visit I preached some about home, and in other places where the people desired me. As I was travelling among destitute churches considerably, the church to which I belonged thought it would be best for me to be ordained, so that I could administer the ordinances of the Gospel where I might be called to preach. Accordingly they called a council for that purpose, and examined me in reference to my Christian experience, call to the ministry, doctrinal views of the Gospel, etc. The council for this purpose was organized by appointing Rev. John Roundy, Chairman, and Rev. Mr. Lord, of Ellsworth, Secretary.

Rev. Benjamin Lord preached the sermon, William Johnson made the ordination prayer, Rev. John Roundy gave the charge, Rev. Edward Carter gave the right hand of Fellowship, and Rev. Ebenezer Pinkham the address to the people. Here I would say that Rev. Mr. Pinkham was appointed to put the usual questions to the candidate before ordination, and this he did, I trust, in a plain and explicit manner. There was one question only that I did not readily answer, and that I did not answer at all. This to me was unexpected and singular. It was as follows: "You believe, brother Norton, that whereas Aaron bore engraved on his breast-plate the names of the twelve tribes of Israel when he went into the most holy place to make an atonement for sin, that Christ upon the cross bore in like manner engraved on his breast the names of all the elect?" To this most remarkable question I concluded in a moment to make no reply, but thought if they did not think proper to ordain me without an affirmative answer to this question, I could not receive ordination. The moderator, however, immediately replied to brother Pinkham and said: "Perhaps brother Norton has not examined that particular subject; you had better pass it by;" and so he did. Every other question being answered satisfactorily, they after a few minutes consultation proceeded to ordain me as I have above stated.

The sermon preached by Rev. Benjamin Lord I thought was an excellent one. The text was 1 Timothy 2:1, which reads as follows: "Thou, therefore, my son, be strong in the grace that is in Christ Jesus." All these exercises were appropriate and solemn. A large congregation witnessed them with apparent seriousness and approbation. This ordination took place in March, 1818, and was noticed in the Baptist Magazine of that number, printed in Boston, Lincoln & Edwards, Publishers.

From this period until April, 1820, I continued to travel and preach in different places the glad tidings of the kingdom of God. By request I made one visit to Machias, and preached at West Machias one Sabbath. Monday evening following I had a meeting in a school house between the two villages. The house was very much crowded. While making my way along through the crowd at the door and in the entry-way, I heard a man say: "How did you like the stranger who preached to us yesterday?" The reply was: "Very well, if he had not spoken so very loud." This put a damper on me for that evening, and in order that they should have no room to find fault on that ground, I spoke quite low that evening, but I enjoyed but little freedom in speaking.

My mother often said I should never do for a public speaker, I spoke so low. This might have been a part of the reason why I did speak rather louder in the beginning of my ministry than public speakers generally do. The first time I visited Mount Desert, after preaching one Sabbath at Pretty March, the brethren wanted me to go immediately to another section of the town and hold some meetings, because, as they said, there was a number of deaf people there who had not heard preaching for years, and they had no doubt but they could hear me with comparative ease. Accordingly I went and held several meetings, in which the deaf folks took a deep interest. But the Machias people had been listening to a Congregational minister, who had a difficulty in his throat so that he had to deliver his sermons in a loud whisper, which somehow increased the contrast between his speaking and mine.

I will here say in reply to the above, that it was then, and still continues to be, my belief that, generally speaking, the loudness or lowness of my voice depends very much on how much of the Holy Spirit's influence I have while speaking.

I attended a meeting while in Machias in a school house opposite what is now called Machiasport one evening, where the people very seldom heard preaching unless they went quite a number of miles for that purpose. After going home with a Mr. Emerson to put up for the night, before retiring to rest, I sung this hymn:

> "How can I sleep while angels sing,
> And all the saints on high
> Cry 'Glory to the Eternal King,
> The Lamb that once did die;'
>
> While guardian angels fill the room,
> And, hovering round my bed,
> Clap their bright wings in love to Him
> Who is my glorious head?"

This hymn had a powerful effect on one of the sons of that family, who has since been converted to the knowledge of the truth, and is now a minister of the Gospel.

I was gone from home on this tour about four weeks. I received fifteen dollars for my services, and paid for horse hire five dollars. I speak particularly of this fact, because the man whose horse I had agreed that I should have him for his keeping.

After this I took another tour to Vinalhaven, where I formed a very interesting acquaintance with several

Ames families. Preached some two or three Sabbaths, and quite a number of evenings. One of those evening meeting was at the house of Deacon Ballage. A circumstance took place in this meeting that I will here relate, though very insignificant in itself it was of some consequence to me. After singing and prayer, having read my text, I proceeded, with a chair before me, to address the people. Having but slight hold of the chair, I noticed a little fellow, perhaps between two and three years of age, leaving his mother and making for the chair. This led me with a firmer grasp to hold on to the chair, but the young urchin staggered along, got hold of it and commenced to tug, he one way and I the other, each endeavoring to have entire possession of the chair. How long this struggle for the chair continued I am unable to say, but I found myself in rather an unpleasant position. To let go the chair would be to throw the boy backwards on the floor, chair and all, and produce quite a sensation in the meeting, get the attention of the people away from the subject I was endeavoring to set before them, and perhaps set my antagonist to screaming at the top of his voice. To retain the chair would be only to exhaust his patience, and the whole thing might pass off unnoticed by most of the congregation. He however gave it up after a while, and went off much dissatisfied with his ill success in his fruitless efforts to obtain the chair.

This was my last visit to this town. I returned to my family, and shortly after preached in the evening at my father's from the words: "The wicked is driven away in his wickedness, but the righteous hath hope in his death" (Proverbs 14 : 32). My brother Thomas, a married man, dated his experience from this discourse. Not long after this his wife also experienced religion. They both became members of the Baptist Church in Brooksville, and have long since gone to their reward. Visited Islesborough again, and baptized a man by the name of Mann. This was the first time that I administered the ordinance to any one. It was on a sandy beach, the water clear as crystal. Being accustomed to the water, I led the candidate off where it was quite deep, and with perfect ease buried him with Christ in baptism. Had a meeting at his house in the evening. A number of young converts spoke, whom I afterwards baptized and added to the church.

The next time I was on this island I fell in with a Free Will Baptist preacher, who soon began to hold meetings. He endeavored to show that the doctrine of predestination, unconditional election, limited atonement, close communion, etc., was all entirely erroneous. His preaching took effect on the minds of the people so that hundreds flocked to hear him. This doctrine I was not at that time prepared to receive, but endeavored to the best of my abilities to substantiate what I believed to be truth. Unpleasant feelings began to arise among the people, hard speeches on both sides were heard, for the people now began to take sides. But notwithstanding all these hindrances the work of the Lord went on, and a great many, especially of the youth, embraced the Saviour. We had frequent seasons of baptizing the young converts. At one of these I recollect of baptizing fifteen. The Free Will brother baptized seven at the same time.

This reformation gave rise to the Free Will Baptist Church in this town; and this whole community, who ever before had been Calvinist Baptists, and well united, with the exception of a family or two of Friends, were now, as it were, shocked right in two, and have remained so up to the present day, and probably will continue so till the ushering in of the millennium day of glory shall unite and make them one in Christ as He is one with the Father. May the good Lord hasten it in its time.

Through fear of my book becoming a larger volume than was at first intended it should be, I shall pass by many things that might have interested the reader, and carry the reader at once forward to the time when I visited Mount Desert the second time.

CHAPTER VII.

In the Spring of 1819 the church at Mount Desert sent for me to make them another visit, which I accordingly did, and preached with them during a number of months to good satisfaction. In the fall of this year I was engaged to keep the winter school in one of their districts called the Cape District. This Summer there was a vessel built near where I used to hold the Lord's day meetings. Happening down on board of this craft one day after she was launched and the masts put in, the riggers being at work on the yards, getting them ready for sending aloft (I said the riggers, for such they were trying to be, but they were only, in lieu of riggers, doing the best they could to put the rigging into its place, it having been fitted to their hands in Boston; (a rigger on Mount Desert was not to be found at that day), stepping forward where the master workman was trying hard to put the peril, so called, on to the fore top-sail yard, I perceived at once that he was puzzled how to pass it round the yard so as to make it come right when the seizing should be passed. Finding himself entirely at a loss, and no one present who could help him out of his dilemma, he says: "Elder, I have heard you preach as though you had been to sea; how do I know now but that you can show me how to put this round the yard?" "Yes," I remarked, "I can show you how to put that peril round the yard, with perfect ease, or any other piece of rigging you have." The fact was, I could rig a ship, and put every block and strap in its exact place with as much certainty as I could count ten. Eleven years on ship board had taught me that business most thoroughly, and nothing to boast of, neither. Could I have preached the Gospel then as perfectly as I could rig a ship, I might have preached it to much greater advantage, and been instrumental in the salvation of many more souls than I could possibly be with all my ignorance and want of education for so great and glorious a work. But to return to the peril. I off coat, rolled up my shirt-sleeves, took the marline-spike out of his hands, and, I wont say in less than no time, but in a time that astonished him for its brevity, had the pevil on and secured in first rate order. The owner standing by, wished to know if I worked at the rigging business now? I told him I worked at anything by which I could honorably support my family. Soon after I saw the owner, Mr. James Fly, and Mr. Richardson, the rigger, in close conversation together. After taking a look at this fine craft, I was about stepping on shore, when the owner wished to know if I would finish rigging his vessel. I told him if he desired it I would, if it would be no put out to him who had undertaken the job. He said it would not, for he desired to be relieved from business he knew so poorly how to perform. Accordingly I borrowed some tarpaulin clothes, and soon had the America, for that was her name, ready for sea.

After this I was frequently sent for to rig new vessels, and did so, always receiving large pay for my services. Sometimes I would go from my rigging business to the pulpit, and from the pulpit to my rigging business.

Late in the fall I commenced my school. This school continued twelve weeks, when it closed, and I went home again to Brooksville.

A number of persons agreed to give me fifty dollars apiece if I would move to Mount Desert the next Spring, which should have nothing to do with my salary, which would be about two hundred dollars yearly. After consulting my family and friends in Brooksville with reference to this important step, I finally concluded to sell out what property I had in Brooksville and purchase a small farm in Mount Desert. This I attended to in the course of the Winter, and when the Spring opened, in the month of April, a vessel was sent in which two of the brethren came, and took on board my goods and what cattle I had, and myself and family arrived at Mount Desert in the month of April, on Fast Day, 1820, where the people turned out, took all my effects on shore, and hauled them up and deposited them in our new house that I had purchased for our residence during our stay upon this island of the sea. I would here observe that this is a large island, perhaps twenty miles long and about twelve broad, containing at that time two towns, Eden and Mount Desert, with, say about three thousand inhabitants.

Here, in the Spring of 1820, I commenced a stated labor in the Gospel ministry. Here I had a good prospect before me, and might have been abundantly useful and successful, no doubt, for many years, and indeed I was measurably so on the whole, but not so much so in this denomination as if I had been thoroughly established in their peculiar doctrines and discipline, as will appear in the sequel of this statement of facts in the case. I have already said in this book that there was a large and somewhat wealthy Congregational Church, whose minister preached in our section of the town a part of the time. But when away, his people would attend our meeting, and especially would they be at our communion seasons.

On these occasions, in giving out an invitation to come to the Lord's table, and receive the sacrament with us, to exclude these good brethren and sisters from the table of the Lord was a hard case, I confess, for me to do, notwithstanding I had no fellowship with sprinkling for baptism, and this condition of things had a powerful tendency to lead some of our members away from close communion. And, in fact, it led me to give this subject a more thorough investigation than I had ever done before.

The result of this investigation will appear from what the reader will find before he gets through with reading this book.

Before consenting to become pastor of the Baptist Church in this place, I had severe trials about it, and prayed for divine guidance in this affair, that if it was my duty so to do, that when I should preach a discourse disclosing my views on the doctrine of the Bible, if the church readily received it as in agreement with their views on the same subjects, I should then conclude it would be right for me to take the pastoral care of the church. Accordingly I selected a text and prayed over it, and studied it. And then I spoke from it, the Lord helping me with his holy spirit to exhibit such truths as I thought naturally grew out of the subject.

The words of my text on this occasion were: "That I may know him, and the power of his resurrection, and the fellowship of his sufferings, being made conformable unto his death." (Phillipians 3 : 10. I observed that to know Christ in the sense of the text, there must be some correct knowledge of the doctrine he taught, etc.

While delivering this discourse, a lady who was a member of the church cried out to give vent to her feelings, which from some cause or other were wrought to the highest pitch of excitement. She finally broke out by saying that I must forgive her for the interruption. I immediately replied that it was no interruption, and said to her, " Free your mind in your own way; and if any other person present wishes to speak they can do so now, or at the close of the meeting, whichever suits them best."

After finishing my discourse, and giving liberty for others to speak, several arose, one after another, and spoke as though they were well satisfied with the discourse.

Not long after this the church received me as their pastor, which solemn and responsible relation to the church I continued to sustain for about eight years, after which it was discontinued. The reader will here find an exact copy of a letter received by me, some years after I had left the Baptists and become a Free Will Baptist, from the Rev. C. P. St. Clair, a Baptist minister then on the isle of Mt. Desert.

"MOUNT DESERT, Dec. 29, 1847.

"To REV. L. NORTON.—*Dear Sir:*—In accordance with your request, I have examined the records of the Baptist Church in this town, and the first time your name is mentioned is under date of Nov. 25th, 1820. At that time, it seems, you were received to the membership of the church by letter. At the same time you, by a vote of the church, received the pastoral charge of the church. At a church meeting, March 30th, 1827, ' Elder Norton acknowledged that he had been unsteady in his principles respecting the order of God's house.' June 7th, 1828, at a church meeting, it was voted, 'That Elder L. Norton be, at his own request, dismissed from the pastoral care of the church.' June 16th, 'Voted That the church cannot any longer approve of Elder L. Norton's preaching under the sanction of this church until existing difficulties respecting his sentiments be removed.' August 12, 1828, 'Voted, To call a Council to advise with the church in its difficulties in Elder L. Norton's case' Sept. 17th, 1828, 'The council convened, and after investigating the case, advised the church to withdraw their fellowship from Elder Norton.' The church, after a season of prayer for divine guidance, voted to accept the report and follow the advice of the council.

"Please excuse me for not writing sooner.

"C. P. ST. CLAIR.

"It seems the church had no trial with you, excepting what grew from their disagreement with you in sentiments.

"C. P. S."

The above is a correct copy of Rev. Mr. St. Clair's letter, but the report of the council is not correctly stated, because instead of their withdrawing the hand of fellowship from me first, which is indicated as the report reads above, it was directly the reverse. And I had said so to the church while the council was present with the church, that I already belonged to the Free Will Baptist Church of Christ, and that I was driven to the necessity of leaving them, that is, the *Calvinist Baptist Church*, on the sole account of their errors.

So that the report of the council, in order to be truthful, should read, and it did read, "That whereas Rev. Lemuel Norton has withdrawn the hand of fellowship from us, we withdraw the hand of fellowship from him."

Soon after this my companion followed me in this same manner, and united with the Free Will Baptist Church of Christ in Mount Desent, of which I was then pastor. The only reason why we did not apply to the church for a regular dismission was because we knew it was contrary to their rules to give a dismission, unless it was to be dismissed to join a church of their own faith and order. What their practice is at the present day I am not prepared to say; probably it is the same.

I will here say the only reason why I left the Baptist was because of what I considered their errors. I always loved them, and I love them still; and had they been as liberal in their faith of the doctrine of the

Gospel fifty years ago as I think they now are, I have no doubt but that I should have remained with them to this present day. I never was a sectarian, never can be. I would not, that I know of, turn my hand over to alter my condition, or to have my choice about what sect I should be of, at the judgment of the great day.

This much I am certain of, that in every nation and in every denomination, he that feareth God and worketh righteousness is accepted with him.

Again, before leaving this subject, I would further say, that I have not brought it before the reader on account of any ill will or bad feelings that I have towards any individual, or any church or denomination of Christians whatever, but merely to give the reader a fair statement of the facts which led to a separation between me and the Calvinist Baptists, with whom I remained some fifteen years from the time I united with them in a church capacity, and should have continued with them to this present day had it not, as I have before stated, been owing to a difference in our views of the doctrine of grace.

And now I am about to relieve the reader's patience from this subject, I want to be indulged one moment longer while I give a word of advice to any into whose hands this little book may fall, who have never united with any sect. Be sure, after you have obtained a good hope through grace, to find a home in some church; but before uniting with any one endeavor to become acquainted first with what you believe yourself, and then with the creed and discipline of those with whom you unite, for be assured that it is no small thing to go from one denomination to another for a home. It has cost me many a sorrowful hour, though I have never seen a moment since I removed my relation from the Calvinist Baptist Church to the Free Will Baptist Church that I was sorry for taking this step, because I know I did it for the truth's sake; yet strange to tell, by so doing I have made of those I took to be my very best friends the most severe and censorious of all my foes.

Soon after I commenced preaching free and full salvation for every creature, I was requested to visit a certain island of the sea called Gott's Island, where there might be eight or ten families residing. When I stepped out of the boat I felt as though I could hardly endure the loneliness of the place long enough to hold a meeting. However, I consented; and the man I was with, being a member of the same church I had withdrawn from, sympathized deeply with me, believing just as I did concerning the doctrine of grace, sent his boys round among the people of the place and notified a meeting at four o'clock in the afternoon. I also called on the Congregational deacon who lived on this beautiful spot of God's earth, surrounded as it was by the mighty deep.

I told him Christ had come on to the island to visit the people, and that there was to be a meeting at four o'clock, at a house, where there were two very aged people lived, who could not get out to meeting, and that we should be glad for him to attend.

While saying this he seemed astonished, and the goad stick seemed to fall out of his hand to the ground. He stepped along and unhooked the chain from the yoke, and let his oxen go to the barn. He was harrowing in his wheat. I followed him to the house; in the house I was told that there was a young lady in the parlor who was sick who they thought would like to see me. She came out directly, and such another object of despair I have seldom ever seen. " Have you been out of health some time?" I enquired. She replied, "About three days." "I should think your mind was somehow depressed; is it not?" I enquired. As I said this, I saw big tears rolling down her cheeks and I could but weep when I thought what sin had done even to youth. I asked her if she felt herself to be a sinner. She said that was what troubled her. Her mother and grandmother spoke highly of her, but it only seemed to increase rather than to allay her grief. I spoke of the meeting in the afternoon, and left, weeping as I passed from house to house, I felt already willing to stay on the island, for I perceived that Christ was there before me, and I loved to be where there was a good deal of weeping among the people, for I had been in the habit of weeping some considerable myself in those days, and I seemed somehow just fit to be among poor sinners who were weeping for their sins, and mourning Christ's love to know.

Oh, what sympathy my soul felt for these!

The meeting commenced at four. The deacon was there and the sick young lady was also there; people from neighboring islands were there. My text on this occasion was from Titus 3 : 4: "But after that the kindness and love of God our Saviour towards man appeared." After showing how and when this loving kindness appeared, and speaking of the greatness of his love, I tried to persuade my hearers to love God in return. Just as I attempted to do this the Holy Spirit descended with such power upon me that the only relief I could find was to speak with all my might, and by so doing for a few moments I found relief, but my hearers were bathed in tears; and what astonished me more than that was that seven young persons had already got upon their knees and were crying for mercy, and confessing what great sinners they had been and still were. Perceiving this, I took my seat, and let them entirely alone. The deacon of whom I have before spoken wanted me to say something to comfort or encourage them. I thought best to let them take their own course, and let the Lord work, for I knew it was the Lord; and surely the Lord did work mightily. After crying in this manner some fifteen or twenty minutes, they arose and took their seats, and I sang that beautiful old revival hymn "The Lord into his garden comes," etc.

The next day several of these found peace in believing and joy in the Holy Ghost. I had meetings every day for four days in succession, during which time sixteen precious souls had been born again, and commenced a new life in the service of the Lord.

There being no church on these outer islands, I

thought it would be best to have one. Accordingly I consulted the most prominent men of the place, and with their concurrence took the necessary prerequisite steps to accomplish such a purpose. There being no Free Will Baptists within some forty or fifty milles of us, it became necessary for me to leave them for a season and go and get such help as was needed to organize a church. Accordingly I left them, went home to see to my own affairs there, and started to inquire for a people called Free Will Baptist. In the town of Lincolnvile, Waldo County, I found a Free Will Baptist Church, and a minister by the name of McKenney, who very kindly furnished me, not only with means of conveyance to Montville, where I found two Free Will Baptist ministers dwelling in one house, namely, Rev. Ebenezer Knowlton and Rev. John True. To these two good men I told my story, to all of which they listened with thrilling interest. I told them I wanted one of them to go with me to those islands, to assist in organizing a church. But they said there was no call for that; — they would take the responsibility of giving me a letter authorizing me to preach, baptize, and organize churches wherever I thought it would be for the glory of God and the good of souls so to do.

Taking my leave of these two servants of God, for such I surely believed them to be, I made the best of my way back to my family, and then to those whom I so fondly loved in the Lord.

I found that during my absence from them they had

continued their meetings, and that the work of the Lord was still going on in the place and spreading to many other islands of the sea.

In my absence other ministers had visited these young converts, and given them an opportunity to join them, but it availed nothing: not one of them could be persuaded to take a step, but in this respect remained just as I left them.

We soon after this had several seasons of baptizing, and happy seasons they were to our precious souls. I baptized several heads of families, and younger persons, down to the age of eleven years.

Here let me speak a few words of the experience of a little girl by the name of Mary Putnam, who in giving a very interesting account of the work of the Lord in what he had done for her soul. Said she, " I was going to the spring one morning for a pail of water." She had been reading where God is represented as as being " more willing to give the Holy Spirit to them that ask Him than parents are to give good gifts to their children," and it came into her mind to try and see if the Bible was true. She said she desired the Holy Spirit more than anything else; accordingly at the spring she knelt down and prayed earnestly for the holy Spirit, and in a short time it so overwhelmed her and filled her so full with love to God and and love to everybody else, that she arose and returned to the house, praising the Lord, and saying to her mother as she entered the house, " Mother, the Bible is true! the Bible is true!"

A day being appointed for the purpose, we met at the dwelling house of a Mr. Thurston (who is now keeper of the light at Bass Harbor), and there proceeded according to the rules of the Free Will Baptists to organize a church of that denomination, who made choice of Bro. Francis Gilley for their deacon and Bro. Richardson for their clerk.

This powerful work extended to about all the islands on this part of the coast of Maine, — to Swan's Island, to Precensha, to the Cranberry Islands, to Tremont, to Barr Island, and to many other places in the County of Hancock.

I frequently visited this little church while I remained an inhabitant of Mount Desert, and preached and administered the Lord's Supper to them from time to time. But after a few years some died, others moved away into the country, and finally the church became extinguished; but there are those who were once members of this little branch of ·God's Zion who are now members of other Free Will Baptist churches, who will never forget the happy seasons they enjoyed in communion with God and each other while they came around the table of the Lord in this place.

The next place where I labored successfully in this great harvest of souls, was on the Cranberry Island, now known as the town of Cranbury. Here God poured out his Holy Spirit, and a goodly number of souls was brought to rejoice in the God of their salvation Among these was a young married lady by the name of Abigail Spurling, whose husband was master of a brig then on a voyage to Belfast, in Ireland.

A day was appointed for baptizing the converts. Nine went forward the first baptizing season we had. Sister Spurling was the first who went into the water — indeed, she was the first who was baptized by immersion in this place. Some said her husband would be angry with her for taking this step, and they hardly knew what he would do to me on his return home. But it proved directly to the contrary, for on his being informed, where he was, of what had taken place at home, he wrote back to his wife that he was very glad to learn that she had become a Christian, and wanted her to pray for him. I will just say that on his return, hearing her relation of what the Lord had done for her, he immediately commenced seeking the Lord for himself, and became a follower of Christ, to the great joy of his worthy companion.

I had several seasons of baptizing here. The work seemed mostly to prevail among the youth, though there were some of all ages who turned their feet to the Lord's testimonies, and became pious. These persons mostly united with the church before spoken of, but their advantages were but few so far as the means of grace were concerned, though they had plenty of this world's goods. I believe the Methodist circuit preacher visits them occasionally.

The next place where my labors seemed to be blest to the good of souls was at a section of the town of Mount Desert then called the Beach, or Otter Creek, since called Tremont. Here the Lord visited the people, and the word preached profited them, being mixed with faith in them that heard it. Here I baptized quite a number, and organized a small church. The day on which I baptized the largest number I preached a discourse on the subject of baptism, and then repaired to the water, where I baptized all who had told their experience and had been received as candidates for baptism. The Holy Spirit was poured out on the assembly in such copious effusions here at the water's side, that it seemed as though they were all about to be converted to God. Dry eyes were hardly to be seen in the congregation that lined these banks of Jordan. At this season I baptized a youth by the name of Lorenzo Gott, who is now an able minister of the New Testament, who graduated at the Bangor Theological School, and, if I mistake not, is now preaching at Ellsworth.

One instance I would like to relate in reference to myself on this occasion, to show the reader the peculiar state of my mind at times, and my great anxiety for souls while laboring in this place. After returning from the water and having taken some dinner, the people soon began to assemble for another meeting, according to previous appointment. My text was, in the afternoon, " How long halt ye between two opinions?" At the close of the discourse Deacon Laud arose, remarking that he had an answer to the question proposed in the text, and that was, " No longer." Numbers of others spoke and praised the Lord, so that it was thought best to let the meeting go on, and if any wished to leave they might leave, and those who wished to stay might remain. The meeting continued till eleven o'clock at night, and then by general consent it closed and the people went home, singing and praising the Lord as they went. The particular incident to which I wished to refer was the fact that after arriving at the house where I went to stop for the night, the lady of the house began to prepare for supper. I enquired why she did so. Said she: " I am getting you some supper." I told her I needed nothing except a little sleep, when she replied: "You have taken nothing since to-day noon; I should think you needed something by this time." I was very much surprised at this, and puzzled to know how it was possible for all that time to pass away so unperceived by me. I told the sister I was glad to perceive that she thought more about me than I did about myself.

Returning home once more, I attended to some business of importance to my family.

In this place let me say, that I had forgotten to speak of the little church that I first organized — I mean about our joining the Montville Quarterly Meeting. It seems by the letter before me that this took place September 20th, 1828.

That the reader may the better understand how my connection was formed with the people called Free Will Baptists, I will here say, what I ought to have said before, that immediately after organizing the said church, they appointed delegates to attend the Montville Quarterly Meeting, and myself being pastor of the church, was of course one of them. We took a boat and started in good season to attend the Quarterly Meeting, to be holden in Prospect, in a new meeting-house, just finished for that purpose. We arrived in due season, presented our request to be received as a sister church, and was by a unanimous vote of the Quarterly Meeting Conference received to the fellowship of that ecclesiastical body, and received the right hand of fellowship as a church in regular standing in that denomination. For the further information of the reader about how I became a member of that denomination, I will here transcribe the entire letter, which now lies before me, and signed by the Clerk of the Quarterly Meeting.

PROSPECT, SEPT. 20, 1828.
Whomsoever it may concern:

This may certify that the Elders of the Montville Quarterly Meeting, in conference assembled, having faithfully examined Elder Lemuel Norton, of Mount Desert, relative to his sentiments and views as a minister of the Gospel of Christ, do find him in sentiment fully united with us in the following things:

First — That salvation is free for all the human family by repentance toward God and faith in Christ, together with humble obedience until death.

Secondly — That the communion of the Lord's supper, in memory of his sufferings and death, should be liberally opened to Christians of all orders in good standing.

Thirdly — That we take the Scriptures of the Old and New Testament as our rules of faith and practice.

Being satisfied that brother Norton has been called of God

to preach the Gospel, and as he received ordination, and remained a number of years a member, of the Maine Eastern Association, in the Calvinistic Baptist Order, we have this day given him the right hand of fellowship, and received him as a member in fellowship with the Elder's Conference, as a Minister of the New Testament. Whereby we commend him to the public, to preach the Gospel and administer all its ordinances.

     Signed,   JOHN TRUE,
           Quarterly Meeting Clerk.

I remained on the Island of Mount Desert about six years after becoming a Free Will Baptist, during which time there was a Free Will Baptist Church organized in my own house, by Rev. Samuel Whitney, of Dixmont, of some fifteen or sixteen members. John C. Somes was appointed deacon, Shubael D. Norton, clerk. This church, I believe, still lives, though I should think it is very feeble at the present time. Some of its members having died, and others having moved away, and being surrounded with so many opposing influences, it would not be at all strange if it should run entirely down and be dropped from the connection. By looking at the Register for 1861, I perceive it has not become extinct, but that it belongs to the Prospect Quarterly Meeting.

In order that my book may not become too large, and exhaust the reader's patience, I shall little more than give a few brief extracts from my Journal while living at Mount Desert after uniting with the Free Will Baptists, although I travelled much in the country, attended a great many of their Quarterly Meetings, notwithstanding I sometimes had to walk sixty, seventy, or eighty miles on foot to get where they were holden.

Sometimes I would take a horse, but then the difficulty of getting off and on to the island, and the danger was so great, that I almost shrank at the idea of taking a horse, as there was no bridge to the island in those days.

In order that the reader may form some idea of my manner of life while travelling and preaching the Gospel, I will here give an account of one of my tours from the island into the country and home again:

Mount Desert, January 28th, 1833.— Taking my wife with me, we left home and rode to the Widow Somes's, between the hills. *Tuesday, 29th,* crossed the narrows and dined at Trenton; put up at Ellsworth; had a meeting in the evening; text, "Let us lift up our hearts with our hands to God in the heavens." *Wednesday, 30th,* arrived at brother Harding's, in Prospect, and had a meeting in the evening. *Thursday, 31st,* preached in a school house near brother Harding's in the evening; very cold about this time. *Friday, February 1st,* visited from house to house. *Saturday, 2d,* attended conference. *Lord's Day, 3d,* spoke to the people from John 3 : 16; in the evening had a meeting at brother John Grant's. *Monday, 4th,* called at Rev. David Swett's; a meeting at the new school house, near the town house. *Tuesday, 5th,* went over to Swanville; stopped at brother Ricker's. *Wednesday, 6th,* stopped at brother

Cunningham's. *Thursday, 7th*, snow storm; meeting in the evening at brother Parsons's. *Friday, 8th*, a meeting at brother Smart's; very cold; rode to Belfast and returned in the afternoon. *Saturday*, had a conference at brother Nickerson's. *Lord's Day, 10th*, meeting in Swanville; meeting in the evening. *Monday, 11th*, rode over to George's settlement; put up with Rev. John Clark. *Tuesday, 12th*, severe snow storm; meeting in the evening at new school house. * * * * Several pages are lost, so that I have to pass to *Feb.* 22d, had a meeting in the evening at brother Mudgett's; enjoyed much life and power in this meeting; the brethren were well engaged. *Saturday*, 23d, rode over to the shore; stopped at Captain Sears Harding's for the night. *Lord's Day*, spoke again to the people in this place; had a third meeting, at brother Samuel Harding's; very stormy during the night; roads blocked up, and very cold. *Monday*, 25th, cold and blustering; felt quite satisfied with the ways of God; meeting in the evening at Mr. Daniel Goodel's; text, " Holiness without which no man shall see the Lord." *Tuesday*, 26th, crossed the Penobscot at Bucksport, in company with brother Harding, and stopped all night at Captain Keyes's, in Orland. *Wednesday*, 27th, snow storm; rode over to Mr. Trueworthy's and tarried all night. *Thursday*, 28th, arrived in Trenton and stopped over night. *Friday, March 1st*, crossed the narrows on the ice; took dinner at brother Somes's, between the hills; got home at four P. M. Found all well, having been absent thirty-three days, during which time we experienced much rough weather, and quite a number of severe snow storms, and received many kind, encouraging words from the people, and felt satisfied that we had endeavored to do the best we could to persuade men to be reconciled to God, and to build up the kingdom of God among men.

On December 18th, 1834, I took another tour into the country. Stopped between the hills to have my sleigh repaired, and put up at night at Captain Thomson's, at the narrows. *Friday, 19th*, crossed on the ice into Trenton, and rode to Orland before dark; attended a meeting in the evening with a newly organized church in this place. *Saturday, 20th*, had a meeting at brother Richardson's. *Lord's Day, 21st*, preached at brother Oliver Gross's, and in the afternoon baptized two — one a young married man, and formerly a Universalist, the other an aged lady of seventy-five years; the weather clear and cold; suffered no inconvenience, however, on account of the cold; the Lord was with us of a truth, and we could say: "Christians, if your hearts are warm, ice and snow can do no harm;" preached in the evening to a crowded house, from the words, "One thing is needful." *Monday* following, preached at the red school house on Orland Ridge. *Tuesday 23d*, crossed Bucksport ferry; attended the funeral of a man who, it was said, died very suddenly in a fit of intoxication; put up at brother Haley's, in Frankfort. *Thursday, 25th*, rode to Newburg and stopped at brother Croxford's;

evening cold. *Friday*, called at deacon Emery's, and attended Elders' Conference in the new meeting house. *Lord's Day*, 28*th*, dedicated the house to the service of the great God and our Saviour, Jesus Christ; this was a very good Quarterly Meeting indeed; love and harmony, peace and unanimity, prevailed throughout the entire meeting; this meeting was protracted nine days; many backsliders were reclaimed, and some who never before spoke in a religious meeting, came forward and related what God had done for their souls. *Monday, January 5th*, went to Augusta, taking with me Rev. Ebenezer Allen, of Dixmont, a representative to the legislature; stopped on the way at Esquire Rich's, in China, over night. *Tuesday, 6th*, took dinner at Augusta; left brother Allen to assist in making laws and statutes for the State, while I went on preaching the glad tidings of the kingdom of God; a tedious cold day this; stopped all night with Rev. Mr. Prescott, a Christian Baptist preacher — rightly named, too, for he received me very kindly. *Wednesday, 7th*, passed over to Wales and attended Quarterly Meeting with the Bowdoin churches; heard some excellent preaching on Wednesday and Thursday. *January 8th*, arrived at brother Noah Norton's, in Bowdoin; found his family well, but, alas! how disappointed, when told that he had been absent about a fortnight, on a visit to Brooksville. *Friday, 9th*, had a meeting in the school house in brother Noah's district. By request of some Congregational brethren, preached in their meeting house on the Sabbath, at

Litchfield Corner. *Lord's Day evening*, preached with my brother's people; this was a highly interesting meeting, no doubt in part on account of my being a brother to the man that they set so much by as their minister. *Monday, 12th*, attended a meeting in company with brother Robinson and a brother Richard Kelly, of Gardiner, in a school house near brother Cook's. *Tuesday, 13th*, attended a meeting at Rev. brother Robinson's, in Richmond. *Wednesday, 14th*, crossed the Kennebec on the ice, and went to Woolwich; attended their conference; had a meeting in the evening at the Widow Gould's; text, "The righteous cry, and the Lord heareth them, and delivereth them out of all their troubles" (Psalms 34 : 15). *Thursday, 15th*, writing this Journal, at brother Tebbetts's. *Friday, 16th*, meeting in the meeting house. *Saturday, 17th*, still in Woolwich. *Lord's Day, 18th*, preached in Wiscasset village. *Monday evening*, meeting in Woolwich. *Tuesday, 20th*, the protracted meeting commenced in Woolwich; spoke to the assembly from the text, "There is that scattereth and yet increaseth," etc.; brother Pinkham, Calvinist Baptist, preached in the evening. *Wednesday, 21st*, brother Kelly spoke from the words, "He that hath friends must show himself friendly;" in the afternoon, spoke from the words, "We then, as workers together with Him, beseech you also that you receive not the grace of God in vain;" in the evening brother Bridges spoke from the words, "All thy works praise Thee, O, Lord, and thy saints bless Thee;" this meeting continued a number of days, and was greatly blessed to the good of many souls. *Friday*, 23*d*, passed over to the Windsor Quarterly Meeting, holden in Whitefield. *Saturday*, a meeting in the meeting house; brother Otis Bridges preached. *Lord's Day*, 25*th*, brother Hobbs, of Augusta, a member of the legislature, spoke to the people in the morning; in the afternoon I tried to preach from the words, " For the grace of God that bringeth salvation," etc.; this was a profitable season. *Monday*, 26*th*, returned to Woolwich. 27*th*, at brother Tebbetts's once more; prayer meeting in the evening. *Wednesday*, 28*th*, had a meeting at brother Seth Hathorn's, in Woolwich. *Thursday*, 29*th*, crossed the Kennebec on the ice, and put up at brother Wakefield's, in Gardiner; spoke in the evening in his school house, from 1 John 3 : 14. *Friday*, snow storm; rode to brother James Parker's, in Litchfield, in company with brother Kelly and Rev. brother Meader, and put up for the night, during which there was much rain. *Saturday*, 31*st*, stormy; attended conference in Gardiner with the Third Church. *Lord's Day, February* 1*st*, preached in Gardiner; text, "That ye would walk worthy of God, who hath called you to his kingdom and glory" (1 Thess. 2 : 12). *Monday*, 2*d*, had a meeting in the school house near brother Goodrich's, in Gardiner. *Tuesday*, 3*d*, at brother Ring's. *Wednesday*, 4*th*, a meeting in Gardiner, near brother Wakefield's. *Thursday*, 5*th*, in company with brother Kelly, went up the river on the ice, to Augusta, where a protracted meeting had been in progress some days; stopped at brother Greenlief's. *Friday, 6th,* had a good meeting in the court house. *Saturday, 7th,* a meeting in the town house in connection with the Calvinist Baptists. *Lord's Day, 8th,* meeting in the town house, and another in the school house. *Monday,* rode to China; preached in the evening at the Chapman school house. *Tuesday, 10th,* preached in a school house at Montville. *Wednesday, 11th,* arrived at Belfast, and put up at Deacon M'Donald's. *Thursday, 12th,* left Belfast, and stopped in Swanville, at brother Smart's; took dinner at brother Ephraim Grant's, in Prospect; crossed Bucksport ferry at sunset; put up at brother Higgings's, in Orland. *Friday, 13th,* journeyed on to Ellsworth, and took dinner at brother Jordan's, a Calvinist Baptist brother; in the afternoon, rode to the narrows, and with some considerable difficulty, together with the loss of a part of my harness, I once more found myself on this great mountainous isle of the sea; drove on to brother Isaac Somes's, in Somesville, and put up for the night; high winds from the south west, with some rain, which ended with some slight flurries of snow. *Saturday, 14th,* harnessed up once more, and started for home; bad sleighing, to be sure, but who regards that when one is bound home. Almost home! oh! how sweet is that little magic word, home! Who can comprehend what is contained in that one word of only four letters, especially when applied to heaven, sweet heaven. At ten A. M. Dick turned up to the gate, entered the dooryard, and stood before the door with all that gladness which it is possible for an unintelligent being to have.

I thanked the good Lord who had been with me in all these journeyings, both by night and by day, and I humbly trust my labor has not been in vain in the Lord. I was absent on this tour fifty-eight days, and the reader will perceive that I was not idle, but as much as in me was, I preached the Gospel of Christ, anywhere and everywhere, where there was an open door for that purpose.

The Lord had taken care of my family during my absence, and none but those who know what it is to go forth weeping and bearing precious seed, understand the joys of those who, after being separated for a season for the kingdom of God's sake, are in his kind providence permitted once again to greet each other on the shores of time.

I have now given to the reader a fair sample of the home missionary's life while travelling and laboring for the the good of souls. And I was just now thinking of the foreign missionary, who has left all for the sake of the kingdom of God, not only for a few weeks or months, but has taken a final leave of all that was dear to him in this world, and has crossed the great broad sea to carry the glad tidings of salvation to those poor souls who have never heard of the Lamb of God that taketh away the sins of the world.

I was just thinking, I say, how entirely unspeakable will their joys be when, after a life of privation and toil in the cause of God, and for the good of souls, they shall meet their death-divided friends in that bright world of glory, where parting will be known no more.

It may be that I have already said as much about my labors in the ministry while I was a resident of the isle of the sea, as I ought to say. Yet there are many things I should like to say before I speak of my removal from this place. I believe I have already said that in consequence of my change of sentiments, not a few of those who before this were very friendly, both of Baptists and Congregationalists, became exceedingly severe against me, and seemed to watch every opportunity they could to get something out of which to make capital to my disadvantage.

But the good Lord was with me, and I have found Him stronger than all those who were against me.

My anxiety for the salvation of souls in the time of the great revival here, which gave rise to the Free Will Baptist cause and the Methodist cause, in 1828, was very great. I could hardly rest day or night. I saw clearly that sinners were in danger every moment of losing their precious souls, unless they fled for refuge to the ark of safety, which is Christ. And I still view them in danger. I then proceeded in perfect harmony with such a view of their dangerous conditions. God sent me to warn them of their danger, and God blessed my efforts and crowned them with abundant success, so that many precious souls were through my instrumentality prevailed upon to seek the Lord while he might be found, and to call upon Him while he was near.

I do not say this by way of boasting, for I have nothing to boast of any more than the pen I now hold in my hand, and write with, has something to boast of because I use it to write with. My object in trying to preach Christ's Gospel is now and always was to save souls. I do not say to save souls from hell in the sense that some seem to understand it, though that may be included in my motive in some respects of the word; but my object was to alarm sinners, to show them, as I have before stated, their danger, and to prevail on them to let their sins go and come to Christ, that they might have eternal life.

In my opinion, the way to save sinners from hell is to save them from their sins. This done and there is no fear of hell or anything else. Let sinners get rid of their sins, and they are at once out of hell and into heaven, as it were.

But some said I was too violent about it. I deny the charge; who could be too violent who was pulling folks out of the fire? Now this was my work; God sent me, not to play with sinners, not to trifle with them, but to pull them out of the fire of sin as fast as possible. And he told me how to do it; and I have no doubt that if every person had minded their own business, I should, by the help of God, have got more out of the fire than I did. But I shall certainly praise God to all eternity for the success I have already had in this great work of saving souls.

Some said I was insane; I did not know but that it might be so, and in order to settle this point, if possible, I took slate and pencil one day and thought I would try a sum in fractions. I concluded an insane person could not be a good mathematician. I found no difficulty, the sum proving perfectly correct. But then, I had a surer touchstone of sanity than figures are, and that was the change, or rather the fruit of that change, that appeared in the lives of those who professed to experience religion under my labors in the ministry. The swearing man left off swearing, the drinking man left off drinking and became a sober man, the Sabbath breaker, who before conversion would visit the rum shop on the Sabbath, was now found in the sanctuary, listening to the voice of wisdom. The worldly-minded man, who was trying so hard to get an abundance of this world that he could hardly leave his labor on the Sabbath, now made every preparation necessary to attend meeting on the Sabbath; and time would fail me to speak of all the glorious triumphs of God's grace in this day of his power among the people.

One of the most remarkable meetings that I now think of, was at a place called Norwood's Cove, which is now in Tremont. This began at four o'clock in the afternoon, and continued till very late at night. In the first place, I preached a discourse from the text, "And to know the love of Christ, which passeth knowledge, that ye might be filled with all the fulness of God" (Eph. 3:19). I then gave liberty, when the Congregational minister arose, seeing the weeping and even trembling in the congregation, observed, "This is nothing more nor less than the power of God; and I," said he, " have always told you that nothing short of his power could bring about a reformation in this place;" he then took his seat. All who wished to be prayed for were invited to manifest it by rising, when a large portion of the assembly rose; they were then requested to pray for themselves, which they accordingly did.

In a short time some who fell on their knees and cried for mercy arose to their feet and praised the Lord, and commenced warning others, so that it was difficult to discern between those who were crying for mercy and those who were praising the Lord for his goodness and his wonderful works to the children of men. It was a season never to be forgotten. No one appeared to be disposed to say aught against it, every one believing it to be the work of the Lord. At a late hour this wonderful meeting broke up, and the congregation dispersed to their several homes to get some little rest. I had perhaps twenty or thirty rods to go, and then immediately retired and attempted to compose my mind to sleep, when the cock crew, and in a few minutes more I perceived the light of day coming in at the window. I perceived there was no sleep for me that night, neither did I wish for any; my cup of joy was full to the brim. This was the first and only night in which I was kept awake all night for the good of souls. It was a blessed night to me. I have often thought of it with satisfaction — one whole night for him who continued all night in prayer to God for me. Oh! that love. I am glad that that mighty Champion of the Gospel, St. Paul, said that it passeth knowledge.

> "Oh! his love, what tongue can tell!
> My Jesus hath done all things well."

I soon arose and retired for secret devotion, but my mouth was filled with his praises. I had meat to eat that the world knew not of. Twenty-two, it was charitably hoped, in that meeting, passed from death unto life, who afterwards united with the Church of Christ, and became living epistles of the truth known and read of all men. Some of them have long since passed over Jordan to their reward, and some remain with us to this present day.

Passing over a great many interesting incidents that took place during my stay upon this island, I will call the attention of the reader to some of the reasons why I moved my family into the county of Waldo. The first of which was, that it is so remote from the people with whom I had become associated. It was attended with too much difficulty to get off and on to the island at all seasons of the year. And another thing, I was getting on in the journey of life so far that I began to be more timid about going from island to island in small boats. And then I thought if I moved off, some younger man might move on and take my place. Another consideration I will name, I had here borne the heat and burden of the day in establishing the doctrine of free and full salvation for every creature whether they will receive it or not. That is to say, if any are lost it will not be because there was not provision made for them in the covenant of grace, but simply because they would not accept of it on the terms of the Gospel. I say, having by the grace of God been enabled to fully establish this glorious doctrine of free and full salvation for every creature, without money and without price, and having lived down the calumny and falsehood heaped upon me for introducing the Free Will Baptist faith and discipline, I felt a desire to move where the people of my own choice were more numerous, and more known as a people of the Lord. From these and various other considerations that might be named, I came to the conclusion that if it should please the Lord to open a way for me, I would move off into some other field of labor, where I might perhaps be more useful than I could be on this rather remote island of the sea.

Accordingly, on the first of September, 1835, I left home and went in pursuit of a small farm and destitute church, where I might farm it some and preach some, and in this way support my family and do some good in the cause of Zion.

After travelling over a number of counties in the central part of the State, and finding nothing that in every respect suited my ideas of a good place for me and my family, I finally returned, having accomplished nothing, except that I had the privilege of preaching to many whom I had never before seen.

Now to make short this part of my history, I would

just say that, having disposed of my farm and settled up my worldly affairs so that I owed no man anything, I put my effects and my family on board a good little schooner of about fifty tons burden, William Gott, Master, and told him to steer westerly, and to put into the first river that he should come to, having a fair wind for that purpose.

Accordingly, the next day we found ourselves sailing up the Penobscot, and in a few hours were made fast to the wharf in Belfast. Here we hired a house and remained some weeks, while I was finding a place to locate my family where they would not be learning the vices of a city life.

Montville, in the County of Hancock, proved to be the place for me. Here I purchased a small farm of about fifty acres, which I greatly improved by my own industry and what help I received from the people.

Here I was, a plenty of good land, producing twenty bushels of the very best of wheat, forty bushels of sound corn, and two hundred bushels of potatoes to the acre, with a good young orchard, plenty of apples and cider, and wood of every description in abundance. To this place I came in the month of October, 1835, being then fifty years of age, and able to do as good a day's work on my farm as I wanted any other man to do.

This might fairly be called a Free Will Baptist town. In it there were three if not four F. W. B. churches: the one where I had settled down was destitute of a minister. In this town dwelt Rev. Ebenezer Knowlton and Rev. John True. Here was the place where the pious and devoted Elder John Colby labored and toiled for souls, and saw the salvation of God marvelously displayed in the conviction and conversion of many souls through his instrumentality.

Here I commenced preaching statedly every Sabbath, according to the wishes of the church and the people. This church was small and very feeble. Universalism had done its nefarious work here; — some had been ensnared with it, and had become the worst enemies the church had to cope with. Some had died, and numbers had moved out West. One thing always puzzled me in reference to this people, and that was this, that Montville is one of the very best farming towns between the two rivers — that is to say, between the Penobscot and the Kennebec; the soil is excellent, always rewarding the husbandman abundantly for his labors, and yet there is more emigration from this town than from any other in the State of the same numbers of inhabitants.

It was not long after moving into this place before I began to think that I must travel and preach the Gospel in other towns also. Accordingly, I furnished myself with good means of conveyance, and when it was consistent with my other engagements to leave home, I did so, and went from town to town, visiting and encouraging destitute churches, and in some places organizing new ones.

My manner of getting along was, when at home, to do up my work as fast as possible, then leave and be absent a number of days, sometimes a number of weeks, and then return and work early and late to make up for lost time, and then away again to attend some yearly, quarterly or protracted meeting. This, to be sure, was a hard way of living, but hard as it was, I could devise no other way for me to do. To leave off preaching altogether would not do; there was an inexpressible woe attendant upon that course, besides guilt of conscience that I could not and would not endure. Had I taken this course, and given up the ministry altogether, I might have supported my family with comparative ease, and in affluent circumstances. This, as I said before, I could not conscientiously do. If I gave up farming, my family must suffer for the necessaries of life, and certainly to leave them to suffer would be denying the faith and becoming worse than an infidel. So here I was, like the colt spoken of in the Scriptures, tied between two ways, the family pulling one way and the suffering condition of the churches and perishing condition of sinners the other way. Now, what is to be done? If the people to whom I have preached had done their duty, I should have been relieved at once. But in most cases where I have travelled they have seemed to ignore the fact that they who preach the Gospel should live of the Gospel.

While a resident of this town, I preached in Belmont, and baptized a number of persons, and organized a church there, which still belongs to the Montville Quarterly Meeting. I. B. Kimball is their present pastor. In Lincolnville, Appleton, Belfast, Prospect, Swanville, Palermo, Freedom, China, Rockland, Thomaston, Warren, Knox, Brooks, Thorndike, Jackson, Washington, Liberty, and perhaps scores of other towns in and out of the County of Waldo, but it will do the reader no good to hear of all my particular ramblings over the State of Maine.

In 1838, the last day of the year, we were called to part with our second son. He was lost at sea, while mate of a brig, of which his elder brother was master, the first day out from Wilmington, N. C., bound to the West Indies. While securing one of the anchors to the bow of the vessel, a sea struck him and washed him overboard. Every possible effort was made to save him, but it was impossible. The wind blowing very hard at the time, and the brig going through the water at the rate of nine miles to the hour, he had to be left, as many a young man has had to be, to make his grave in the boundless deep. He was a young man of much promise, having obtained a good education, in part at Readfield Seminary, and at other places. This was the greatest affliction that we had ever met with. My poor wife, I think, never got entirely over this. There was but one alleviating circumstance about this bereavement, and that was, Lemuel was prepared to go. Sudden and dreadful as was his death, and though an indescribable loss to us, to him it was gain. He experienced religion when but nine years of age, in the time of a powerful work of the Lord in Mount Desert. While the evening sacrifice of prayer and praise was being offered up to God, while on his little knees by his father's side, his soul first breathed the vital air of life divine, and felt the love of God shed abroad in his child-like heart. I shall always be thankful to God for that mercy, because he converted him to the knowledge and acknowledgment of the truth when but a mere child. Oh! how precious the thought, to think that while that young man was struggling with death in the midst of the foaming billows, his Saviour's eye was upon him, angels commissioned from the throne of the Eternal were there hovering over him, ready, as soon as the last struggle was over, to receive his released spirit on their wings and bear it home to the paradise of God

This was the first inroad that death had made into our family of ten children, and a fearful breach it was — never to be made up to us in this world, though my companion bore it with Christian fortitude and calm submission to the divine will.

There was one little incident not wholly unconnected with the events of the sad day that brought us the tidings that our son was lost, that seems worthy of remark. A few days previous to this, I had received an invitation to preach at the house of a Universalist, from the text: "And other sheep I have, which are not of this fold; them also must I bring, and there shall be one fold and one shepherd." My appointment had gone out to preach that very evening, according to request. Not being willing to disappoint the people, I attended according to promise, and explained the text as well as I could under those circumstances, and I believe to the general satisfaction of all present.

I used frequently to give temperance addresses at the different places where I was called upon thus to do.

In 1848 I was again, in the providence of God, called to taste deep of the bitter cup of affliction, by having to part with my companion, with whom I had shared the joys and sorrows of life nearly forty years, and had brought up a family of ten children, the youngest being about sixteen years of age when his mother died.

The following extract of a brief notice of the death of my wife is copied from the Morning Star of March 29th, 1848, a religious paper printed in Dover, N. H.

Died in Montville, Maine, January 18th, Mary, wife of Rev. Lemuel Norton, in the fifty-eighth year of her age. Sister Norton experienced religion in 1813. She was baptized by Rev. Lemuel Jackson, and united with the Baptist Church in Sedgwick, and, together with her husband, remained with the Baptists fifteen years, after which they both renounced the doctrine of a limited atonement, unconditional election, close communion, etc., and joined the Free Will Baptists, believing as they do, that the atonement was designed as much for one person as another, and that the only reason why some are saved and others lost is, because some obey the Gospel while others reject it. She continued with the Free Will Baptists till removed by death to the church triumphant. Being brought up by a pious grandmother, she was taught the fear of the Lord from a child. The prominent traits in her character were as follows: An even temper, always mild and pleasant; industrious, always usefully employed; a keeper at home, only when duty called her away; the Bible, Sabbath, and Sanctuary, she considered as rich legacies from her heavenly Father; her faith in the promises was unwavering; her attachment to and care of her own family was great, and that without the least indifference to the welfare of others. In a word, her happiness consisted in communion with God and in doing good. The last thirty-five years of her life was an even-spun thread of holiness to the Lord. But she has left us. Having finished her course, and kept the faith, she rests from her labors, and her works they will follow her. At her funeral a very large concourse of people attended, when a solemn and appropriate discourse was delivered by Rev. Ebenezer Knowlton, in which Rev. T. B. Robinson and Rev. Ezekiel Fogg took part, from the text, Proverbs 14 : 32, "The righteous hath hope in his death."

CHAPTER VIII.

In the April following this sad bereavement I broke up house-keeping, and sold at public auction about everything I possessed except my farm, and removed to Belfast, where I stopped but a few months, and then began again to travel and sound the glorious Gospel to perishing sinners.

Very unexpectedly one day, while attending some evening meetings in Boothbay, I fell in with my youngest son, Thomas Norton, who informed me that he would rather not go to sea any longer, but wished me to return to Montville and commence keeping house again. And principally for his sake, as he was a youth of about seventeen, I consented; and in the fall of 1848 I again returned to Montville, stocked my farm anew, and went on life's journey as well as I could. But I soon found great difficulty arise from the want of some one to keep the house. I hired the best of help, to be sure, but in two cases out of three, some one else, whom I knew nothing about, had more control over them than I had, so that when I wanted them most they would be off I knew not where. This made it unpleasant. My daughters were either married or away trying to do something for themselves, except the youngest, who about this time returned from the city of Belfast, where she had been living, in the family of a highly respectable gentleman by the name of H. O. Alden, Esq., in a state of partial derangement, occasioned by having the typhus fever a few weeks before. This was my third great trial, and such a one as but few parents have to pass through in this present world. After remaining at home about fifteen months, and becoming rather dangerous, it was thought best by all concerned, for her to go the hospital at Augusta. Accordingly, on February 5th, 1850, I took her with me to the hospital, where she continued, with but two short intervals, for six years.

During my daughter's residence at the Insane Hospital, I was travelling and preaching in different parts of the State of Maine, and in this way I found many families who were struggling to support their insane friends at the hospital. This led me to inquire into the equality of that law which virtually deprived, in in a great measure, the poor of the benefits of the hospital, and favored the rich, on account of their money, to be sure, with all its benefits. In consequence of this view of the subject, I obtained of William Munger Esq., Counsellor at Law, of Portland, a petition for the people to sign, asking a change in the Maine Insane Hospital Law so far as for the State to pay the expenses of the poor at the hospital, that they might be be continued there instead of being thrust into a miserable almshouse. there to be neglected, and to perish for want of that very care and attention which the hospital so abundantly provided. In 1856 this petition was granted in part, so that the State now pays one dollar a week for those who are unable to pay their own bills.

On December 13th, 1848, death made another call, and took another of my children, Lydia Jane Norton, wife of David Norton, Jr., son of David Norton, Esq., of Montville. She left two small children, the youngest of which was three months old at the time of her death. Her death was triumphant indeed. As I entered her room about three hours before she expired, she said to me: "Dear father, your prayers and exhortations have kept me from committing many a sin, but you must not be surprised if I have a number of hard struggles with death before I get through." But contrary to her expectations, she had none. The last words she uttered were: "This bed, which felt so hard a few days ago, now feels like a bed of down."

In 1850, May 11th, another dear daughter was suddenly taken from her little family, leaving to deplore their loss, a husband and five small children, the youngest of whom was but twenty hours old when its fond mother closed her eyes upon all things earthly.

Time rolls on; days, months, and years, pass rapidly by, like swift ships, in quick succession.

November 22d, 1849, I was married to my second wife, whose maiden name was Sophronia Averell, of Alna, Maine, with whom I am now living.

After returning home from a tour, in which I visited Boston, and many other towns in New England, we removed from North to South Montville, where I built a small dwelling house and remained about two years.

Before this, several of my children having moved to Falmouth, County of Cumberland, I concluded, for their sake as well as my own, to sell out and make one more move, in order to be near my children when it should please my Heavenly Father to call me to that home from which there will never be any occasion for removing.

Accordingly, after selling my house to the good brother who built it for me, namely, Joseph Fogg, Esq., I took a team and started for the cars in Gardiner, and on the 27th of May, 1856, we arrived at our new home, in Falmouth, where we have lived ever since, it being just five years next month.

Since my arrival here, after preaching a short time in the City of Portland at the almshouse, I have travelled and preached more extensively than ever — in New Hampshire, Massachusetts, Rhode Island, Connecticut, New York, and Philadelphia, mostly in Seamen's Bethels.

June, 1860, took a tour to Acton, Maine; took the cars to North Berwick. *June 5th*, passed over the road to Lebanon; stopped at brother Ricker's. *June 6th*, when within two miles of the meeting house in Acton, while ascending a steep hill, our horse, which was very smart, took fright by meeting a cow with a piece of board over her eyes, and turning suddenly around, threw me out with such great force as almost to dislocate my neck. The good Lord saved me for some purpose, I hardly know what — to write this book, it may be. While attending the Quarterly

Meeting in this place, I had the privilege of stopping all night with brother Farnham, who was in his one hundred and fifth year, and who is the last of the survivors who were present at the battle of Bunker Hill; and what astonished me was his strength and activity, attending the meetings like any gentleman of seventy-five or eighty. *June 8th*, arrived in Biddeford. *Lord's Day*, 10*th*, preached to the Cedar-street Church. 11*th*, took a walk through the cotton mills. *June* 12*th*, went down the river in a sail-boat to the Pool, so called; fifty-eight years ago, when but a youth, I visited this place; only two or three houses here then — now it is quite a village; went up into the top of the light-house on Wood Island; could see Cape Elizabeth and Boone Island in the distance; Mr. Bryant, who keeps this light for three hundred and fifty dollars a year, has every thing in good order in this place; at two P. M. returned to the Pool, and had a meeting in the evening at the school house; subject, "Preciousness of Christ." *Thursday, June* 14*th*, returned to the city; very warm to-day. *Lord's Day*, 17*th*, preached for the Unitarian Church in Kennebunk; stopped at the Massum House. 19*th*, attended the Yearly Meeting in Wells; had rather a rainy time, though a very interesting meeting. *Friday*, 22*d*, rode down to the beach, a distance of six miles; returned at night and stopped at Senator Wells's, whose great-great-grand-father was the man for whom this town was named; brother Wells had a son at the Maine State Seminary who was injured by falling from a swing so that he died soon after. *Lord's Day*, 24*th*, preached for the Calvinist Baptists to day; had a pleasant time with them. *July* 1*st*, preached for the Free Will Baptists in Wells. *Monday*, returned to Portland; stopped over the Fourth; went to the fireworks, which were very splendid. Returned home on the fifth, having been absent one month.

Having given the reader a very brief summary of some of my journeyings from place to place while engaged in the great work of travelling and preaching the Gospel, I shall now draw towards a close of this work, by a few extracts taken from my journal while on a tour to New York and Philadelphia, in the summer of 1860.

Being somewhat at leisure about this time, I thought I would go and visit these cities out of which I used to go to sea when a youth, not knowing but that I might possibly recover something of the wages which I earned while on board the ship Concord, of Philadelphia, which was lost on the coast of Florida, after being taken by a British man-of-war.

Accordingly, on the ninth of August, 1860, I went on board the steamer Patapsco, for New York, and arrived there the tenth; in the afternoon crossed the ferry to Jersey City; put up at the Philadelphia House. 11*th*, took the cars for Philadelphia; arrived at one P. M; took lodgings at the Widow Galloway's, 27 1-2 North Second-street. *Sunday*, 12*th*, heard Rev. Mr. Hutter deliver a discourse; subject, "Perils in the City." *Monday*, 13*th*, very warm;

went to the Custom House and examined the records of Clearances of Vessels for 1803 and 1804; could find no account of the ship, but here I made a mistake — it was in 1805 that I was cast away in the English sloop-of-war Fly. Stopped in the city a few days, and preached in the Seamen's Bethel. *August 15th*, walked down to the Navy Yard; saw several men-of-war; the steam frigate Powhattan, lying in the river, had just arrived from China, by the way of Rio, having been absent fourteen months, and, as it was said, had rendered much service to her country. *Thursday, 16th*, took the cars this morning, and arrived in New York at eleven A. M. — just in season to attend the Fulton-street prayer meeting; saw the Great Eastern lying in the North River; preached in the Seamen's Bethel in the evening, for Rev. Mr. Steward, Baptist. *Friday*, visited many parts of the city, especially the Free Will Baptist Meeting House, which is a most thoroughly built church, and in a very popular part of the city, containing many convenient rooms in the basement for the convenience of those whose privilege it may be to occupy them; took dinder with the Rev. Mr. Moulton, present pastor (Rev. Mr. Graham being now in Europe), at brother Winch's, in Horatio-street; at five P. M. took passage in the steamer Commonwealth, of New York, for Stonington; thank the Lord for relief from the noise and bustle of the great metropolis of the United States. *Lord's Day, 19th*, preached in the Baptist Church in Stonington; subject, "Joy in heaven over one sinner that repenteth," etc.; in the evening spoke to the colored church. *Monday*, 20*th*, took the cars, and at eleven A. M. arrived in Providence; found brother Day not at home; took my trunk to Deacon Kelly's, 78 Night-street; called to see Professor Hayes, at Olneyville. *Tuesday*, 21*st*, attended a meeting in Olneyville. 22*d*, went to Greenwich, and attended a funeral in company with brother Baker, a Baptist Minister; in the evening preached at the Baptist house in East Greenwich. *Thursday*, 23*d*, took the cars again for Providence, and called on Rev. Dr. Wayland; at three P. M., on board the Bradford Duffee, for Fall River; very showery to-day; preached in the evening in Fall River. *August* 24*th*, took the cars, and arrived at New Bedford at ten A. M.; preached in the evening in the Missionary Bethel. 25*th*, at Taunton. Preached at Taunton on the Sabbath for Rev. Mr. Gowen, Free Will Baptist. *Monday*, 27*th*, at Sailors' Home in Boston; all night at Dr. Enoch Osgood's. 28*th*, very pleasant; preached at the Sailors' Home, in Purchase-place. 29*th*, at a prayer meeting in the Old South. Made a few remarks in reference to Christ's power and willingness to save sinners. One night in Charlestown. *Thursday*, 30*th*, went to Milford; David Norton's family gone to Montville; went to East Boston; saw my son-in-law, David Norton; took dinner with Rev. Mr. Cox, Methodist, and returned to Purchase-street Sailors' Home, and at five P. M. took steamer for Portland. Arrived home *August* 31*st;* found all well, after being absent twenty-two days, during which time I experienced much of the loving kindness of the Lord, and much sympathy of friends and strangers.

Since my return from Philadelphia I have been travelling and preaching in different places in the State, and find myself somewhat infirm on account of my advanced age.

I have come to the conclusion that it will be as well for me to close this memoir by giving a few words of advice to the youthful readers. I am aware that it is much easier to give good advice than it is to receive and obey it. But I will here offer a few thoughts for the benefit of those who may chance to read this book, after its author has passed to that bourne from whence there is no return.

And in the first place, I would advise you to be exceeding cautious how you contract any bad habits at any time of life, especially while you are young. If you should, when you come to be of maturer age, and find them destructive to your happiness and well-being in this life, as well as in that which is to come; you will perceive that it is almost impossible for you to get rid of them; they will grow with your growth and strengthen with your strength, till they become incorporated into the very texture of your soul, and become a sort of second nature to you, and be as difficult to overcome as though they were born with you and in you. Therefore, see to it that you successfully resist the first approach of temptation to do any thing wrong. And when and wherever you are at a loss to know what is right and what is wrong, let conscience and the Bible settle the matter; they will generally agree, and when they do they are invariably right.

Again, the wicked one is always busy with youth; the strength of his kingdom depends very much upon the youthfulness of his subjects. Oh! let lovely youth beware of his devices. He begins with little — it may be to take an apple as you pass them on the sidewalk — it may be some other trifling thing that does not belong to you — no matter how insignificant the article, his object is to make you a transgressor of God's law. I do not think that Satan expects to make at once a thorough and finished sinner of any youth, but he tries, if possible, to sow the seeds of sin in youthful hearts before the seeds of grace are sown; and to frustrate his wicked designs, let all young people, if possible, attend the Sabbath School.

And finally, let every one seek first the kingdom of God and his righteousness, and all good things shall be theirs.

SERMON.

UNTO YOU, THEREFORE, WHICH BELIEVE, HE IS PRECIOUS.
—1 *Peter* ii. 7.

Whatever is precious is costly — is of great price. Gold is precious — partly because of its scarcity, and partly on account of its great usefulness among men. Diamonds and pearls are precious, too, on account of their intrinsic value; but none of these are so precious as Christ.

He is precious whether we believe on Him or not. Our faith makes no alteration in Christ. He is the same yesterday, to-day, and forever. Faith in Christ changes our relation to Him and his relation to us; that is to say, if we believe in him, He becomes our Saviour, and we become his children, his friends, etc.

In discoursing briefly from these words, I shall attempt two things. First, to show wherein the preciousness of Christ consists; and, Secondly, What is to be believed in order for Christ to become precious to us as individuals.

First: Christ is precious. And why? Because He is God. He is one of that Holy Three that bare record in heaven — the second person in the Trinity — and in God over all blessed forevermore.

To quote all the Scripture that goes directly to prove this fact would far exceed my limits. I shall, therefore, only name a few which I consider right to the point. John 1:1, "The Word was with God, and the Word was God." John 1:3, "All things were made by Him, and without Him was not anything made that was made." Hebrews, 1 : 6, last clause, " And let *all* the angels of God worship Him." It would be idolatry so to do if He is not truly and properly God, and in obeying God in this particular we should transgress the laws.

Christ is precious because He is the *Son* of God. We do not say that Christ is his own father, as some pretend to say we do, but we do say that He is the Son of the Father, and we say it because the *Bible* says it. Neither do we attempt to say how these things can be We are not required to comprehend these sublime mysteries. It is enough for us to know that it is so, but we have nothing to do with knowing *how* it is so. He is the only begotten of the Father, full of grace and truth — the brightness of the Father's glory — the express image of his Person — always doing his Heavenly Father's will; "This is my beloved Son, hear ye Him." Again, Christ is precious as a man going about doing good — healing all manner of diseases and sickness among the people — causing the blind to see, the deaf to hear, the lame to walk, the dumb to speak — sometimes casting out devils — and even raising the dead to life. Yea, precious is he as a Mediator between God and man ; having two distinct natures, and being both God and man, He is completely qualified to fill the mediatorial office and reconcile the world to God. And this He did by fulfilling the law — magnifying it and making it honorable — and by condescending to be made sin for us, who knew no sin, that we might be made the righteousness of God in Him. His blood is precious — it has atoned for all our race, and sprinkled over the throne of grace.

He is precious in that He is the Lamb of God, that taketh away the sins, not of the Jews only, but the sins of the *world* — opening a lawful door of hope for every repenting, returning sinner, so that none need perish now who will come to Christ that they may have Eternal Life. He is precious in all his offices, as Prophet, Priest and King, as the Way, the Truth, and the Life — as the true Bread that cometh down from heaven, whereof if a man eat he shall never die — as the true Vine, from which all the children of God may draw sap, and nourishment for their souls, so that they may bear much fruit to the honor and glory of God. He is precious because mighty to save to the utmost, and because He is the Author of eternal salvation to all them that obey Him — as the Foundation of the Church of God, and as the chief Corner Stone, uniting Jews and Gentiles in one common brotherhood, and bringing both on to the same savable grounds, so that peace is now preached alike to him that is afar off and to him that is near, so far as Jewish ceremonies are concerned. He is altogether lovely, and the chiefest among ten thousand. As the apple tree is among the trees of the wood, so is Christ among the sons. He is precious as our example of benevolence — became poor, that we might, through his poverty, become rich. As an example of non-resistance — "And was led like a lamb to the slaughter, and as a sheep before her shearer is dumb, so he opened not his mouth." I love to dwell on his preciousness, but time and space fail me. Angels dwell on this theme with delight. They strike their golden harps anew, and sing of his preciousness with joy unspeakable and full of glory. I will add four lines of Dr. Watts's beautiful poetry, and then pass.

> "All over glorious is my Lord,
> Must be beloved, and yet adored;
> His worth, if all the nations knew,
> Sure the whole earth would love Him, too."

Secondly: What we must believe in order for Christ to become precious to us as individuals. First, then, we must believe the Bible. That is, we must believe the doctrines taught in the Scriptures concerning God, and Christ, and ourselves — that God is a Sovereign, and will punish the wicked except they repent — that we are sinners, lost, helpless, undone sinners — and that we are condemned already — and that the wrath of God abides upon us — and that we cannot help ourselves in the least, or make ourselves any better by anything we can do. In a word, we must believe that for us there is no help but in Christ — that he alone can do helpless sinners good. "The whole need not the Physician, but they that are sick." "Christ came not to call the righteous, but sinners to repentance." And before a sinner will feel his need of Christ, or will come to Christ for salvation, he must see that all his righteousness is worthless, and that unless the Saviour becomes his righteousness he has none that will answer the demands of the Divine Law.

When a sinner is brought by the Holy Spirit's influence to see himself exceeding sinful — in a word, when a sinner discovers the Law to be exceeding broad, extending to every thought, and himself to be carnal, sold under sin, it is then, and not till then, that he will truly appreciate the Saviour; and he will then esteem Him more to be desired than gold — yea, than much fine gold. And believing on Him, taking and receiving Him as He is freely offered to us in the Gospel, and having Him formed in the heart, the hope of glory, the soul will be filled with joy inexpressible, and peace that passeth all understanding.

The believer in Christ finds him to be the Lord, our righteousness in every deed; as the prophet expresses it, "He shall be called the Lord our Righteousness," or, as the apostle expresses himself, "Who of God is made unto us, wisdom, and righteousness, and sanctification, and redemption; that according as it is written, he that glorieth let him glory in the Lord."

Now Christ is everything to the believer. He is the believer's *Life, Hope, Joy,* Peace, and Salvation;

in Him he finds all the promises of God to be *yea* and amen. Glory to God.

> How precious is the name, brethren sing,
> How precious is the name of Christ our Paschal Lamb,
> Who bore our sin and shame on the tree.

Having, in short, spoken of the preciousness of the Saviour, and what we must believe in order for him to be so to us, I will try to improve this subject by persuading sinners to come to this blessed Saviour, who has done and suffered so much to save their precious souls.

He who thought it not robbery to be equal with God, made himself of no reputation, but took on him the form of a servant, and came into this wicked world on purpose to save sinners. Oh, come then to the friend of sinners! He is anxious to save you, every one of you. He pities you. Oh, come! give yourself up into his hands; He will wash all your sins away, and teach you how to watch and pray, and live rejoicing every day. Do not let the wicked one persuade you that it is time enough yet. "Delays are dangerous;" "Procrastination is the thief of time." If the wicked one can prevail on youth to put off the concern of the soul for the present, his object is gained — this is all he cares about. He knows if he can keep you along in this way, and lead you on step by step to form bad habits while you are young, that they will grow with your growth and strengthen with your strength, and that he will have you so entirely in his power that it will be nearly impossible for you to break away from him, or to recover yourself out of his cruel snare.

The Saviour calls you, dear sinner, oh! listen to his sweet charming voice. Oh! hear him saying, "Ho, every one that thirsteth! come ye to the waters, and he that hath no money come; yea, come, buy wine and milk without money and without price."

Once more before I die, dear sinner, as I have gotten almost through life, and almost through this book, and almost through this short sermon, oh! let me once more in Christ's stead beseech you to let all your sins go. Flee to Christ, who is the ark of safety and city of refuge for your poor soul. And let the author of this book, poor as it may be, have the unspeakable pleasure, if not in this world let him in the judgment of the great day, have the amazing joy of knowing that as far as you are concerned he has not labored in vain, nor written these pages in vain.

And, in conclusion, I will ask my Christian friends especially, and also all others into whose hands this book may chance to fall, in reading it to remember that the author was seventy-six years of age when he wrote it, and of course had to omit the insertion of many incidents which would no doubt have been highly interesting to the reader, for want of recollection of these events so clearly as to render them satisfactory to his own mind.

> Come, chidren, learn to fear the Lord,
> And that your days be long,
> Let not a false or spiteful word
> Be found upon your tongue.
>
> Depart from mischief, practice love,
> Pursue the works of peace;
> So shall the Lord your way approve,
> And set your souls at ease.

FINIS.

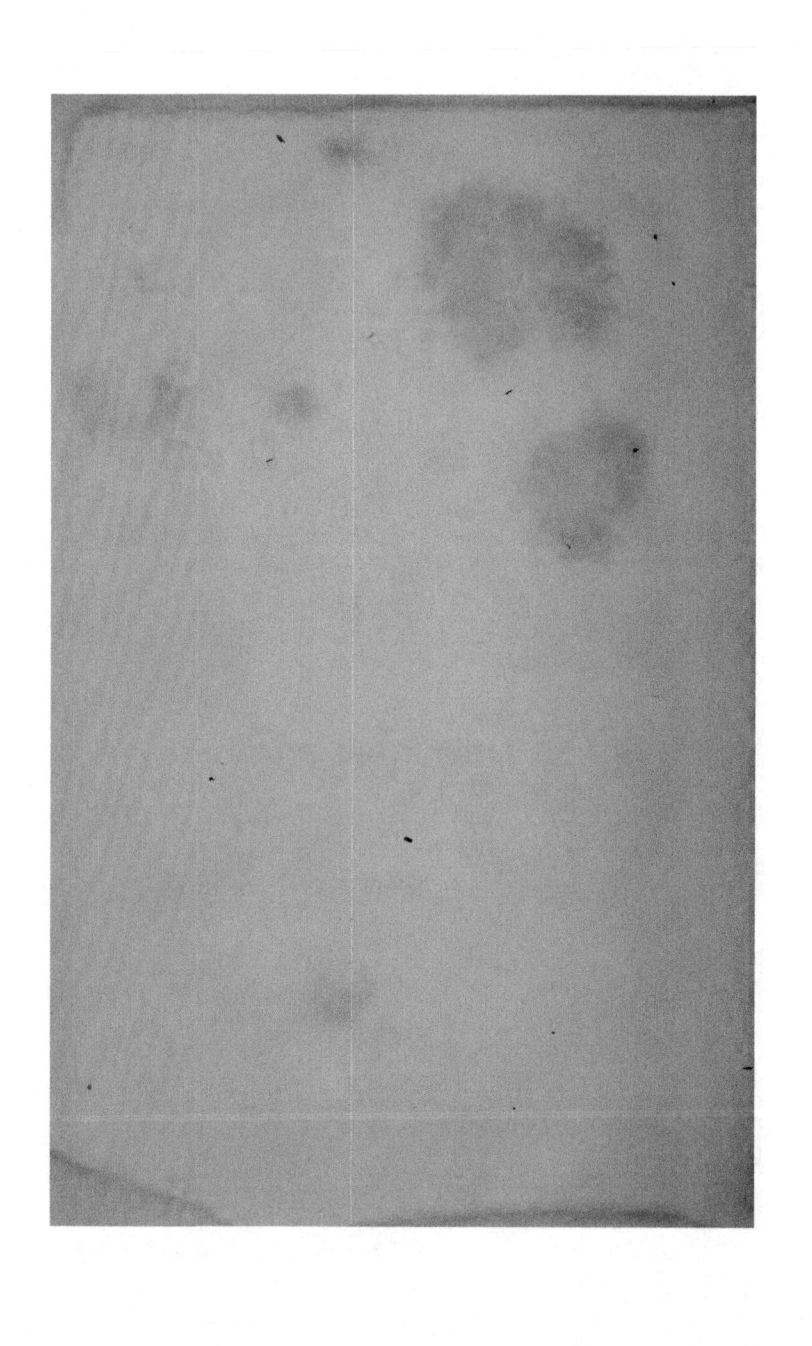

DATE DUE			
GAYLORD			PRINTED IN U.S.A.

		922.6 N825a
Norton, Lemuel		
AUTHOR		
Autobiography		
TITLE		

DATE DUE	BORROWER'S NAME

922.6
N825a